Spiritual Lessons

for Growing Believers Workbook

Bible Basics from A to Z

Keith D. Pisani

WESTBOW
PRESS®
A DIVISION OF THOMAS NELSON
& ZONDERVAN

WestBow Press books may be ordered through booksellers or by contacting:

WestBow Press
A Division of Thomas Nelson & Zondervan
1663 Liberty Drive
Bloomington, IN 47403
www.westbowpress.com
1 (866) 928-1240

ISBN: 978-1-4908-9387-7 (sc)
ISBN: 978-1-5127-6328-7 (e)

Print information available on the last page.

WestBow Press rev. date: 12/18/2019

CONTENTS

INTRODUCTION

Spiritual Lessons for Growing Believers Workbook is a "spiritual birth to spiritual maturity" interactive study series for new and maturing Christians. The study begins with a four-session follow-up study for new believers (published also as a separate booklet titled *Spiritual Lessons for New Believers* and available through the author's website at www.keithpisaniministries. com). Once a new believer has completed his initial follow-up studies, he participates in two transition studies *(Baptism Class* and *Membership Class). Bible Basics from A to Z,* the third study, is published by WestBow Press and is available through the author's website at www. keithpisaniministries.com. Packed with information that leads to transformation, this series of twenty-six thorough studies helps growing believers become mature in Christ. The answers for the exercises found in this workbook are given in the content of the workbook's companion book, *Spiritual Lessons for Growing Believers* (published by WestBow Press and available through the author's website at www.keithpisaniministries.com). An additional book in the series is awaiting publication.

Believers need to grow (1 Peter 2:2; Hebrews 5:14; 2 Peter 3:18). God wants believers to practice their faith and get from where they are to where they need to be. At the time of this writing, all or parts of *Spiritual Lessons for Growing Believers Workbook* have been used in nine countries to help thousands of believers grow in Christ (United States, Canada, Liberia, Togo, Ghana, Grenada, Great Britain, Israel, and Russia). This study has helped new believers qualify for leadership positions in the local church and has equipped them for participation in ministries of service. Believers who have used these studies have become church officers and missionaries on home and international fields. This is a high-impact study that God can use to change your life. Also, it is a series of lessons that can be used in any teaching context: church services, Sunday school, small groups, Bible studies, personal and group devotions, chapels, college and seminary classrooms, adult Bible fellowships, Christian schools, homeschooling sessions, and elsewhere.

May God bless the lives of all who study God's Word for the purpose of growth. My prayer is that all who participate in *Spiritual Lessons for Growing Believers Workbook* will practice the "Word-centered" life. Enjoy the study.

Promoting the "Word-centered" life,
Keith D. Pisani

PROGRESS REPORT

Please record your progress in the *Spiritual Lessons for Growing Believers* course. I have attended the instruction time and have completed the study sheets for the following study sessions:[1]

1. follow-up (1)	___Yes	___No
2. follow-up (2)	___Yes	___No
3. follow-up (3)	___Yes	___No
4. follow-up (4)[1]	___Yes	___No
5. baptism class	___Yes	___No
6. membership class	___Yes	___No
7. assurance	___Yes	___No
8. Bible	___Yes	___No
9. church	___Yes	___No
10. doctrine	___Yes	___No
11. evangelism	___Yes	___No
15. filling and Fruit	___Yes	___No
16. gifts of the Spirit	___Yes	___No
17. heaven and hell	___Yes	___No
18. integrity	___Yes	___No
19. Jesus Christ	___Yes	___No
20. keys to spiritual growth	___Yes	___No
21. last days	___Yes	___No
22. ministries of service	___Yes	___No
23. new nature	___Yes	___No
24. obedience	___Yes	___No
25. prayer	___Yes	___No
26. quiet time	___Yes	___No
27. relationships	___Yes	___No
28. stewardship	___Yes	___No
29. trials	___Yes	___No
30. unity	___Yes	___No
31. victory	___Yes	___No
32. worship	___Yes	___No
33. x-ray	___Yes	___No
34. yielding to God	___Yes	___No
35. zeal	___Yes	___No

---

[1] The four follow-up sessions are published separately under the title *Spiritual Lessons for New Believers* and can be obtained through Keith D. Pisani's website at www.keithpisaniministries.com.

36. perspectives on discipleship　　　　　___Yes　　　　　___No
37. the practice of discipleship　　　　　___Yes　　　　　___No

Name of participant: _____

Course completion date: _____

SPECIAL NOTES

The answers to the fill-in-the-blank sections of this workbook are found <u>underlined</u> in the companion book *Spiritual Lessons for Growing Believers,* which is published by WestBow Press and available through the author's website at www.keithpisaniministries.com. All scripture quotes are from the King James Version of the Bible.

SPIRITUAL LESSONS FOR GROWING BELIEVERS

Follow-Up (Initial Four-Session Bible Study for New Believers)

FOLLOW-UP

Just as physical babies should not be left on the doorstep to fend for themselves, neither should spiritual babies be left to grow on their own. Paul's approach to discipleship was "as a nurse cherisheth her children: so being affectionately desirous of you, we were willing to have imparted unto you, not the gospel of God only, but also our own souls, because you were dear to us" (1 Thessalonians 1:6–7). The early church cared for new converts as a mother cares for her newborn baby. Should the modern church do less?

Follow-up is the initial phase of discipleship. Follow-up begins after a person receives Christ as Savior. The salvation experience may take place inside the church at an "altar call," in a classroom, through a children's ministry, or during a harvest event. A person may come to Christ and experience regeneration outside the church during an outreach event, one-on-one or group evangelism, with a believer, or apart from a believer in the privacy of a person's one-on-One time with God. Wherever salvation happens, Christians are responsible to initiate follow-up. The purpose of follow-up is spiritual growth toward maturity in Jesus Christ.

Physical babies grow. Babies who do not grow are given special medical attention to promote physical growth. Just as a non-growing physical baby is considered an aberration, it is considered not normal for a babe in Christ to remain spiritually immature. Just as first-century believers grew "in the grace and knowledge of our Lord and Savior Jesus Christ" (2 Peter 3:18), modern believers should grow into maturity for Jesus Christ.

When a person receives Jesus Christ as Savior, a believer who is trained in the four phase 1 follow-up sessions should take the first of those four sessions, give one copy to the new convert, and keep one copy for himself. The believer (now called "the discipler") will take the new convert, open the first session, and review the instructions on the top of the first study. "My name is _____" is the name of the new convert being discipled. "My helper's name and phone number (contact information) are ___ _____" includes the name of the discipler. Both the new convert and the discipler will need a Bible for study and a writing instrument (a pen or pencil) to fill in the blanks and to take notes. The study is keyed to the 1611 King James Version of the Bible.

If both the discipler and the new convert are available, the first session can begin immediately in a private setting. Males follow up males. Females follow up females. Approved workers follow up children. The session is taught or led out loud by the discipler. (Christ said, in Matthew 28:18–19, that "teaching" is an effective discipleship method.) If the first session begins immediately, the discipler and new convert can, at the end of session 1, arrange for a prescribed place, date, and time to meet for session 2. After session 2 is taught or led and completed, the discipler and new convert can establish a prescribed place, date, and time to meet for session 3. The same pattern is true also for session 4.

At the time just after the new convert's salvation experience, if both the discipler and the new convert have a scheduling conflict and cannot begin immediately, the discipler should make an appointment with the new convert and establish a prescribed place, date, and time when both the discipler and the new convert can meet. If no time is available, the discipler can assign the first study as a take-home assignment to be brought back for review, with the discipler, at a prescribed place, date, and time. If this latter arrangement is made, the discipler will review the answers to session 1, make comments, and then teach or lead session 2 to the new convert. At the conclusion of session 2, the discipler can assign session 3 as a take-home assignment, ask the new convert to bring session 3 back for review, and then, after session 3 has been reviewed by the discipler, session 4 can be taught or led by the discipler. Once all four sessions have been completed, the new convert will be asked to enroll in the two transition studies that lead to church membership: the one session baptism class and the one session membership class. Phase 2 (*Bible Basics from A to Z*) follows.

In making disciples, we are not making disciples of ourselves. We are making disciples of Jesus Christ. It is a privilege to serve Jesus in making disciples of new converts, seeing them grow into maturity for Christ.

The four sessions include the reading content of instructive opening paragraphs, fill-in-the-blank questions, matching, some memorization, and some writing. The minimal qualifications needed to use the follow-up materials, as a discipler, are the discipler must himself be a believer and the discipler must be able to read.

May God bless the use of these follow-up studies. They are cross-generational and adaptable to all age groups. At the time of initial publication, the studies have "born fruit" on three continents and in fifteen countries. My prayer is that all believers will grow into maturity for Christ.[2]

---

[2] The four-session follow-up study is published separately in booklet form and can be obtained through the author's website at www.keithpisaniministries.com.

FOLLOW-UP 1
YOUR FAITH IN JESUS CHRIST

My name is _____.

My helper's name and phone number are _____

_____.

Please read the following paragraph out loud:

The person who receives Jesus Christ as Savior is the recipient of many blessings. He is a new creation in Jesus Christ (2 Corinthians 5:17). He becomes a citizen of heaven (Philippians 3:20). He acquires a new inheritance (Ephesians 1:3–14). He is the beneficiary of many promises (John 14:1–3). His salvation is secure (John 10:28–30). The purpose of this study is to review some blessings that accompany salvation.

Read the scripture references given. Then place appropriate answers in the spaces provided.

1.   How does God describe an unsaved person?

He is like a sheep which has gone _____ (Isaiah 53:6).

He is _____ already because he has not believed in Jesus Christ as Savior (John 3:18).

He has _____ _____ of the glory (righteous standards) of God (Romans 3:23).

He will be cast into the _____ ____ _____ because his name is not found written in the book of life (Revelation 20:15).

2.   How does God describe the saved person?

He is _____ _____ (John 3:3, 7). This phrase means "to be born from above (born from heaven)."

He is _____ _____ because he has believed in Jesus Christ as Savior (John 3:18).

He is a new _____ in Jesus Christ (2 Corinthians 5:17).

He is a newborn _____ (1 Peter 2:2).

His sins are _____ because of Jesus Christ (1 John 2:12).

3.   How long does salvation last?

The person who believes in Jesus Christ knows he has _____
(1 John 5:13).

The person who has eternal life shall never _____ (John 10:28).

4.   Who guarantees that salvation will last forever?

The _____ Himself bears witness with our spirit that we are the
_____ of God (Romans 8:16).

The believer is kept (guaranteed salvation) by the power of _____ through faith
unto salvation (1 Peter 1:5).

5.   Read 1 John 5:12. Then answer the following question:

Are you sure that you will enter heaven beyond this life?

_____ Yes _____ Not Sure

6.   Based on your understanding of the Bible, answer the following question:

If you were to die today and meet God, and He should ask you why He should let you
into His heaven, what would you say?

_____

_____

_____

_____

_____

_____

7.   John 3:16 describes how God provided for man's salvation. Make this verse personal.
Please place your name in the spaces provided.

For God so loved _____, that He gave His only
(uniquely) begotten Son (Jesus); that _____ who
believes in Him should not perish but that _____ should have
everlasting life (John 3:16).

8.   Review sections 1–7. Answer the following questions:

Have you received Jesus Christ as your personal Lord and Savior?

_____ Yes _____ No

Are your sins forgiven? _____ Yes _____ No

How do you know that you have everlasting (eternal) life?

9.   For additional study, read each of the following verses and comment on what each of them means to you:

      O   Ephesians 2:8–9
      O   Romans 8:35–39
      O   Titus 3:5
      O   Philippians 1:6

10.   *Our Daily Bread* is one of many devotional study guides. Daily Bible study helps you to grow in your relationship with Jesus Christ. For your spiritual encouragement, be faithful in reading the Bible references and thoughts in *Our Daily Bread*.[3] Or ask your helper to recommend another devotional guide. Read your Bible daily.

11.   First John 5:11–13 reminds the believer that God guarantees eternal life. It is a Bible passage on assurance of salvation. Commit 1 John 5:11–13 to memory. Then repeat the passage, out loud, to a Christian friend.

---

[3]   *Our Daily Bread* is a publication of RBC Ministries (Grand Rapids, Michigan).

FOLLOW-UP 2
YOUR LIFE IN JESUS CHRIST

My name is _____.

My helper's name and phone number are _____

_____

Please read the following paragraph out loud:

The person who receives Jesus Christ as Savior is spiritually reborn (John 3:3, 7). Believers begin spiritual life as "newborn babes" (1 Peter 2:2). It is natural for babies to grow and develop. Believers must "grow in grace and in the knowledge of our Lord and Savior Jesus Christ" (2 Peter 3:18). Spiritual growth requires spiritual nourishment. The believer's primary source of nourishment is the Bible. The purpose of this study is to discover from scripture how believers can grow through regular nourishment from God's Word.

Read the scripture references given. Then place appropriate answers in the spaces provided.

1.   How can believers grow in Jesus Christ?

Spiritual "newborn babies" need the sincere _____ of God's Word that growth might result (1 Peter 2:2).

When spiritual babies become more mature, they can discern more difficult passages of scripture. These scripture passages are called the strong _____ of God's Word (Hebrews 5:14).

God's Word is _____ (John 17:17).

God's Word is alive and powerful and is a _____ of the thoughts and intents of the human heart (Hebrews 4:12).

God gave the Bible. It is profitable for _____, for _____, for _____, and for _____, in righteousness (2 Timothy 3:16).

Believers must be diligent to be workmen who are not _____, rightly interpreting the word of truth (2 Timothy 2:15).

The Word of God's grace is able to make the believer strong (_____
_____) and give you an _____ among all who are sanctified
(Acts 20:32).

2.   How can believers communicate with God?

God communicates His mind to believers through scripture. Believers communicate
back to God through prayer. Prayer is talking to God. Prayer is the genuine believer's
natural response to God (Romans 8:1; 1 John 4–5).

Paul said to _____ _____ _____ (1 Thessalonians 5:17).
Through prayer, believers have immediate access to God. Believers can pray anytime.

Jesus said to _____, _____, and _____ and it shall be
opened to us (Matthew 7:7). God responds to believers who pray.

Believers must make prayer requests in _____ believing that God will
answer prayer (Matthew 21:22).

Believers must ask in the _____ of Jesus Christ (John 14:13). The name of Jesus
is the summary statement of all that Jesus is. By closing your prayer, "In Jesus's name,
Amen," God's Son becomes involved in your prayer (He identifies with your prayer).

3.   For what should believers pray?

Believers should pray for daily _____ (Matthew 6:11), for
protection from being led into _____, and for deliverance
from _____ (Matthew 6:13).

Believers should pray for _____ in dealing with the trials of life
(James 1:5).

Paul prayed for other believers (Romans 1:9). He asked other believers to
_____ for him (Romans 15:30–32).

Believers should pray that others would _____ on Jesus Christ in response
to His Word being spoken (John 17:20).

Believers should pray for all who are in _____ (1 Timothy 2:2).

4.   Begin a personal prayer diary. Include columns to record requests, the date the
requests were made, how God answered those requests, and the date God answered
each request.

5.   David wrote, "Delight thyself also in the Lord: and He shall give thee the desires of thine heart" (Psalm 34:4). Believers must want what God wants. The will of God is a key essential to answered prayer. For additional study, draw lines connecting the following scripture passages to the appropriate references:

The Bible is a weapon known as "the sword of the Spirit."	Psalm 119:105
The Bible is a "lamp" unto our feet and a "light" unto our path.	Ephesians 6:17
The Bible is a "looking glass."	Psalm 126:5–6
The Bible is eternal and will "never pass away."	James 1:23
The Bible is a "precious seed."	Matthew 24:35
The Bible is "sweeter than honey."	Jeremiah 23:29
The Bible is like "fire" to your soul.	Psalm 19:10
The Bible is "milk" providing spiritual nourishment.	1 Peter 2:2

6.   For your encouragement, read your Bible daily, pray daily, and memorize a sequential listing of the books of the New Testament. A sequential listing of the New Testament books is found in the table of contents of your Bible.

The books of the New Testament are listed as follows:

Matthew	2 Corinthians	1 Timothy	2 Peter
Mark	Galatians	2 Timothy	1 John
Luke	Ephesians	Titus	2 John
John	Philippians	Philemon	3 John
Acts	Colossians	Hebrews	Jude
Romans	1 Thessalonians	James	Revelation
1 Corinthians	2 Thessalonians	1 Peter	

(There are twenty-seven in all.)

FOLLOW-UP 3
YOUR WALK WITH JESUS CHRIST

My name is

My helper's name and phone number are

Please read the following paragraph out loud:

Believers have spiritual privileges and moral responsibilities. Believers are the "child[ren] of God" and are "joint-heirs" with Jesus Christ (Romans 8:16–17). Christians can "love one another" (1 John 4:7). A goal for each believer is conformity to Jesus Christ (Romans 12:1–2). The purpose of this study is to describe your spiritual privileges and moral responsibilities.

Read the scripture references given. Then place appropriate answers in the spaces provided.

1.   Believers have the privilege of telling others about Jesus Christ.

The practice of telling others about Jesus Christ is called witnessing (Acts 1:8). If Jesus Christ is worth having, He is worth sharing with others. The Bible has much to say concerning the witness of believers.

Believers must be ready to give an _____ to every man who asks a reason of the _____ that is in you (1 Peter 3:15).

Proverbs 11:30 teaches that "he who wins _____ is wise."

The believer who goes forth with God-given sincerity, bearing the precious seed of the gospel, will doubtless come again with _____, bringing his _____ (new converts) with him (Psalm 126:6).

Acts 1:8 indicates that witnessing for Jesus Christ includes the following four geographical locations: _____ (your community), _____ (your county and state), _____ (your country), and the _____ _____ ___ ___ _____ (internationally to the continents beyond).

The believer has the responsibility to witness to _____ men "of what thou hast seen and heard" (Acts 22:15).

14

2.   Believers have the privilege of waiting for the return of the Lord.

       God's true church is taken to heaven in the rapture (1 Thessalonians 4:13–17).[4] The promise of the rapture gives comfort to true believers (1 Thessalonians 4:18). Then we who are "alive and remain shall be _____ (raptured) together with them in the clouds to meet the _____ in the air; and so shall we ever be with the _____" (1 Thessalonians 4:17).

       Jesus Christ has prepared a home in heaven for those who know Him as Savior. His promise is "I will _____ again" (John 14:3).

       Believers look for "that blessed hope" which is the glorious _____ of our Savior Jesus Christ (Titus 2:13).

3.   Believers have the privilege of pleasing Jesus Christ. This involves guarding against temptation.

       When believers are tempted to do wrong, God provides a way of escape. "There hath no _____ taken you but such as is _____ to man; but God is _____, Who will not suffer you to be _____ above that ye are able, but will with the temptation also make a _____ of escape that ye might be able to bear it" (1 Corinthians 10:13).

       Temptation is a desire to think or do something that does not please God.

4.   Read 1 Timothy 6:6–12. Comment on the passage in the space provided.

       _____
       _____
       _____
       _____

5.   The Bible provides help in determining whether certain activities, attitudes, and thoughts are right or wrong. Match the following scripture references with the appropriate statements:

       Will it glorify God?   1 Corinthians 10:31

       Can it be done for the Lord?   Colossians 3:17

---

[4] Although the English word "rapture" does not appear in the KJV English translation, it is from a Latin term that means "to catch up" or "be caught up."

Can it be done in the name of the Lord?	Colossians 3:23
Is it of that evil world system that opposes all that God represents?	1 Thessalonians 5:22
Are you in doubt about it?	1 John 2:15
Is it good in its appearance?	Romans 14:23
Would it hinder a fellow believer?	2 Corinthians 6:14
Will it form an unequal yoke with an unbeliever?	Romans 14:21
Could it become my master?	1 Corinthians 6:12
Is it God's will for my life?	James 4:15
Am I willing to face it in the Judgment? (Would I want to be involved in this activity when Jesus Christ comes again?)	2 Corinthians 5:10
Do I want to reap the fruit of this activity in my future life or in the lives of those I love?	Galatians 6:7

6. Practice witnessing by sharing Jesus Christ with others. The following is a sample plan of salvation that you can share with a friend:

Romans 3:10; 3:23	All have sinned.
Romans 5:12; 6:23	The consequence of sin is spiritual death which is separation from God forever.
Romans 10:9, 10, 13; John 1:12	Sinners must receive Jesus Christ as personal Lord and Savior.

7.   From the following passages of scripture, in what other activities do believers participate?

   1 Corinthians 16:1–2   Believers g_____ offerings to God.

   Psalm 100:1–2   Believers s_____ the Lord with gladness and p_____ His name.

   2 Timothy 2:15   Believers st_____ God's Word.

8.   Memorize Psalm 119:11. "Thy Word have I hid in my heart that I might not sin against Thee."

   Live in the power of the Lord.

FOLLOW-UP 4
YOUR FELLOWSHIP WITH JESUS CHRIST AND HIS PEOPLE

My name is _____

My helper's name and phone number are _____

_____

Please read the following paragraph out loud:

Believers enjoy fellowship with God the Father, Jesus Christ, and with people who know the Lord (1 John 1:3). Fellowship is the sharing of a common bond with others. Fellowship with other believers must be consistent with the scriptures (Romans 16:17–18). Every believer needs fellowship. The purpose of this study is to examine how believers can enjoy the fellowship God provides. Read the scripture references given. Then place appropriate answers in the spaces provided.

1.   Is church attendance important?

Believers are not to _____ the assembling of ourselves _____ as the manner of some is, but instead to encourage one another through faithful church attendance, because of the Lord's return (Hebrews 10:25).

No one _____ to himself, and no one _____ to himself (Romans 14:7). Believers are responsible for being faithful to God and others.

2.   Believers have a responsibility to be baptized by immersion, following salvation.

Is baptism a step of obedience to the command of Jesus Christ (Matthew 28:18–20)?

_____ Yes _____ No

The Bible records the instructions of Peter to a group of new Christians. "And he _____ them to be _____ in the name of the Lord Jesus" (Acts 10:48).

How important is obedience to the commands of Jesus Christ (John 15:14)?

How much water is necessary for baptism? John the Baptist went to Aenon because_____ water was there (John 3:23).

Is water baptism necessary for salvation (Ephesians 2:8–9)?

_____ Yes _____ No

A helpful class on believer's baptism is offered at the church. Why not arrange with the pastor to attend this class?

3.   Believers have a responsibility to observe the Table of the Lord (communion).

Who instituted the Table of the Lord (Matthew 26:26–28)?

_____ _____.

The bread used in the communion service is *symbolic* of the _____ of Jesus Christ which was given for believers at Calvary (1 Corinthians 11:24). The cup, filled with grape juice, is symbolic of the _____ Jesus Christ shed on the cross for forgiveness of sins (1 Corinthians 11:25). Communion is observed in _____ of what Jesus Christ did at Calvary (1 Corinthians 11:24–25).

4.   Believers have the responsibility to join a local church (church membership).

Acts 2:41–42 lists a sequence of three important events in the lives of new believers. First they gladly _____ the Word (salvation), then they were _____ _____ (by immersion following salvation), and finally, they were _____ (joined as members) to the local church. These early believers formed a local fellowship. They became members of a local church (Acts 1:15).

In review, in what three events did the new believers participate?

a.   <u>Salvation</u>
b.   <u>B</u>
c.   <u>Church Membership</u>

Following the successful completion of baptism class, the church offers a class on local church membership. You are invited to participate in this class.

5.   For your encouragement, review the truths presented in the following lessons:

   O   your faith in Jesus Christ
   O   your life in Jesus Christ
   O   your walk with Jesus Christ
   O   your fellowship with Jesus Christ and His people

Review Notes

6.   For your growth, continue to read your Bible, pray daily, and memorize scripture passages relating to your walk with Christ. Also memorize, in sequential order, the names of the books of the Old Testament. A sequential listing of the Old Testament books is found in the table of contents of your Bible and as follows:

Genesis	Ecclesiastes
Exodus	Song of Solomon
Leviticus	Isaiah
Numbers	Jeremiah
Deuteronomy	Lamentations
Joshua	Ezekiel
Judges	Daniel
Ruth	Hosea
1 Samuel	Joel
2 Samuel	Amos
1 Kings	Obadiah
2 Kings	Jonah
1 Chronicles	Micah
2 Chronicles	Nahum
Ezra	Habakkuk
Nehemiah	Zephaniah
Esther	Haggai
Job	Zechariah
Psalms	Malachi
Proverbs	
(There are thirty-nine in all.)	

ANSWERS TO THE FOLLOW-UP SESSIONS
(For the Discipler)

Session 1: Your Faith in Jesus Christ

Isaiah 53:	6astray
John 3:18	condemned
Romans 3:23	come short
Revelation 20:15	lake of fire
John 3:3, 7	born again
John 3:18	not condemned
2 Corinthians 5:17	creation
1 Peter 2:2	babe
1 John 2:12	forgiven
1 John 5:13	eternal life
John 10:28	perish
Romans 8:16	Spirit sons/children
1 Peter 1:5	God

All other answers should be reviewed, on an individual basis, by the discipler with his disciple.

Session 2: Your Life in Jesus Christ

1 Peter 2:2	milk
Hebrews 5:14	strong meat
John 17:17	truth
Hebrews 4:12	discerner
2 Timothy 3:16	doctrine, reproof, correction, instruction
2 Timothy 2:15	ashamed
Acts 20:32	(build you up), inheritance
1 Thessalonians 5:17	pray without ceasing
Matthew 7:7	ask, seek, knock
Matthew 21:22	prayer/faith
John 14:13	name
Matthew 6:11	bread/daily needs, temptation, evil
James 1:5	wisdom
Romans 15:30–32	pray
John 17:20	believe
1 Timothy 2:2	authority

Matching:

The Bible is a weapon.	Ephesians 6:17
The Bible is a lamp.	Psalm 119:105
The Bible is a looking glass.	James 1:23
The Bible is eternal.	Matthew 24:35
The Bible is precious seed.	Psalm 126:5–6
The Bible is sweeter than honey.	Psalm 19:10
The Bible is fire.	Jeremiah 23:29
The Bible is milk.	1 Peter 2:2

Session 3: Your Walk with Jesus Christ

1 Peter 3:15	answer, hope
Proverbs 11:30	souls
Psalm 126:6	rejoicing, sheaves
Acts 1:8	Jerusalem, Judea, Samaria, uttermost parts of the world
Acts 22:15	all
1 Thessalonians 4:17	caught up, Lord, Lord
John 14:3	come
Titus 2:13	appearing
1 Corinthians 10:13	temptation, common, faithful, tempted, way
1 Timothy 6:6–12	(Review the answers individually from the text.)

Matching:

Will it glorify God?	1 Corinthians 10:31
Can it be done for the Lord?	Colossians 3:23
Can it be in the Lord's name?	Colossians 3:17
Is it of the evil world system?	1 John 2:15
Are you in doubt about it?	Romans 14:23
Is it good in its appearance?	1 Thessalonians 5:22
Would it hinder a believer?	Romans 14:21
Will it form an unequal yoke?	2 Corinthians 6:14
Could it become my master?	1 Corinthians 6:12
Is it God's will?	James 4:15
Am I willing to be judged for it?	2 Corinthians 5:10
Do I want to reap its fruit?	Galatians 6:7
1 Corinthians 16:1–2	give
Psalm 100:1–2	serve, praise
2 Timothy 2:15	study

Session 4: Your Fellowship with Jesus Christ and His People

Hebrews 10:25	forsake, together
Romans 14:7	lives, dies
Matthew 28:18–20	yes
Acts 10:48	commanded, baptized
John 15:14	obedience demonstrates we are disciples of Jesus Christ
John 3:23	much
Ephesians 2:8–9	no
Matthew 26:26–28	Jesus Christ
1 Corinthians 11:24–25	body, blood, remembrance
Acts 2:41–42	received, baptized, added
	salvation, baptism, membership

Notes

SPIRITUAL LESSONS FOR GROWING BELIEVERS (TRANSITIONAL STUDIES)

Baptism Class

Membership Class

Keith D. Pisani

BAPTISM CLASS (STUDY GUIDE)

Introduction: Baptism by immersion following salvation is one of the first acts of obedience for every believer. This study takes four plunges into the water of the Word concerning this elementary doctrine.

I.   The Must of Baptism

    A.   Baptism is commanded by Jesus Christ.   Matthew 28:18–20

    B.   Baptism is commanded for the Christian.   Acts 10:47–48

II.   The Mode of Baptism

    A.   The Meaning of the Word "Baptize"

    B.   The Method of Baptism in the Bible

        1.   The baptism of Jesus   Mark 1:9–11

        2.   Baptism by John   John 3:23

        3.   The baptism of believers   Acts 8:36–38

III.   The Message of Baptism

    A.   Baptism pictures salvation.

        1.   Baptism does not save.   Acts 8:12, 36–38; 18:8

        2.   Baptism is a symbol.   Romans 6:3–5

    B   Baptism precedes church membership.   Acts 2:41

IV.   The Manner of Baptism at This Church

Notes

BAPTISM CLASS STUDY HELPS

New Testament Passages on Baptism (all types)

- Matthew 3:6, 7, 11, 16; 21:25; 28:19
- Mark 1:4, 5, 8, 9; 10:38, 39; 11:30; 16:16
- Luke 3:3, 7, 12, 16, 21; 7:29; 12:50; 20:4
- John 1:25–33; 3:22, 23, 26; 4:1; 10:40
- Acts 1:5, 22; 2:38, 41; 8:12, 16, 36–39
- Acts 10:37, 47, 48; 11:16; 13:24; 16:14, 15, 33, 34. 18:8
- Acts 18:25; 19:3, 5; 22:16
- Romans 6:3–5
- 1 Corinthians 1:13–17; 10:2; 12:13; 15:29
- Galatians 3:27
- Ephesians 4:5
- Colossians 2:12
- 1 Peter 3:21

The Meaning of the Word "Baptism" in Greek Lexicons (Dictionaries)

- Liddel and Scott: "to dip in or under water"
- Thayer: "to dip, to cleanse by dipping, to immerse in water, to overwhelm"
- Bauer, Arnt, and Gingrech: "to dip, immerse, dip oneself, wash, plunge, sink, drench, overwhelm"

Comments by Church Leaders

- John Calvin: "The word 'baptism' signifies immersion. It is certain that immersion was the practice of the early church."
- Bishop Lightfoot: "As the (person) sinks beneath the baptismal water."
- Martin Luther: "Baptizo is a Greek word translated 'immerse.' I would have those who are to be baptized to be altogether immersed."
- John Wesley: "Buried with Him in baptism. This alludes to the ancient manner of baptism by immersion."

Baptism Requires	Scripture Cited	Immersion Requires
water	Matthew 3:11	water
much water	John 3:23	much water
going into	Acts 8:38	going into
coming out ofActs 8:39	coming out of	
form of burial	Romans 6:3–4	form of burial
form of resurrection	Colossians 2:12	resurrection

MEMBERSHIP CLASS (STUDY GUIDE)

Introduction: Membership is the commitment of a believer to the fellowship of a local church. Through salvation, the believer identifies with the Person of Jesus Christ. Through membership, the believer identifies with the people of Jesus Christ. This study presents two topics related to membership.

I.   The Christian Who Desires to Join the Church

      A.   Privileges of the Christian

            1.   The Privilege of Being a Member of the Universal Church 1 Corinthians 2:12–14; Acts 5:14

            2.   The Privilege of Becoming a Member of a Local Church1 John 1:3–4; Acts 2:41, 47

      B.   Principles for the Christian

            1.   Requirements for Membership   Acts 2:41

            2.   Responsibilities of the Member   Acts 1:14

II.   The Church the Believer Joins

      A.   Beliefs (ABC's)

            1.   Articles of Faith

            2.   Baptist Distinctives (for Those in a Baptist Church)

            3.   Covenant of the Church

      B.   Bylaws

            1.   Constitution

            2.   Commitment to Missionaries

      C.   Becoming a Member

            1.   Baptism by Immersion Following Salvation

            2.   Membership Class

            3.   Meeting with the Church Leadership

            4.   Motion and Approval by the Church

            5.   Membership

SPIRITUAL LESSONS FOR GROWING BELIEVERS

Bible Basics from A to Z

Keith D. Pisani

A: ASSURANCE

Just as salvation is a work of God, so is the believer's eternal security. From God's perspective, "once saved, always saved" is described as eternal security. From the believer's perspective, the same doctrine is called "assurance of salvation." The terms "eternal security" and "assurance of salvation" are interchangeable. Both terms affirm that salvation is forever. The purpose of this study is to answer three questions about a believer's assurance of salvation.

1.   Assurance of salvation is taught in scripture. It is the confidence that once a person receives Jesus Christ as Savior, he is saved for eternity. What does the Bible say about a believer's assurance of salvation? The following are a handful of the many scripture passages that teach eternal security (assurance of salvation). Look up each passage in your Bible. Then explain each passage in the space provided.

Text/Passage	Explanation of the Text
Isaiah 49:16	
John 5:24	
John 6:37	
John 10:27–29	
John 11:25–26	
John 17:11	
Romans 8:1–3	
Romans 8:16	
Romans 8:29–30	
Romans 8:31–39	
1 Corinthians 1:8	
Ephesians 1:13–14	
Philippians 1:6	

Hebrews 10:4

Hebrews 13:5

2 Timothy 1:12

2 Peter 1:5

1 John 5:11–13

Jude 1

2. Jesus said, "Ye shall know them by their fruits" (Matthew 7:16). Since believers can be "fruit inspectors," what evidences indicate that a person is saved? Using your Bible, look up the following passages from 1 John, identify the believer's evidence of salvation, and write the evidence in the appropriate space provided:

1 John 1:5–7 A genuine believer's life is not characterized by _____ sin.

1 John 2:7–11 A genuine believer recognizes God's _____ in his life.

1 John 2:29 A genuine believer does good _____.

1 John 3:9 A genuine believer does not _____ to yield to temptation.

1 John 3:14 A genuine believer _____God and man with Christlike love.

1 John 4:13 A genuine believer experiences the _____ of God's Holy Spirit.

1 John 5:1 A genuine believer _____ that Jesus Christ is _____.

1 John 5:4 A genuine believer can be_____ by God to live the Christian life.

1 John 5:11–13 A genuine believer has _____ of salvation

3. Although assurance of salvation is presented in numerous scripture passages, many genuine believers continue to doubt the eternal duration of their salvation. From the following passages, what causes believers to doubt their salvation? Look up

each passage in your Bible. Then, from the following list, fill in the blank with the appropriate letter by matching each passage to a potential cause for doubt. (God's teachings on assurance of salvation are never a source of doubt.)

Scripture Passage		**Potential Cause for Doubt**	
2 Timothy 2:12	_____	A.	false teachings that "add to" or "take away from" God's Word
1 John 4:1	_____	B.	the possibility that the individual never received Christ in his life
Revelation 12:10	_____	C.	a worldly lifestyle (continued sin in the person's life)
Matthew 13:22	_____	D.	the liar Satan accusing believers of inconsistent living
Romans 3:4	_____	E.	a failure to take God at His word

4.   For your encouragement, please answer the following questions and complete the following exercises:

If you were to die today, stand before God, and He were to say, "Why should I let you into My heaven?" what would you say?

"You should let me into your heaven because_____
_____
_____
_____

Read 1 John 5:12. Then answer the following question:

Are you sure that you will enter heaven beyond this life?

 Yes   Not Sure

Evaluate your salvation experience. With zero percent meaning you do not know if you are saved and with 100 percent meaning you know beyond a shadow of a doubt that you are saved, on the following line place an X at the appropriate place on the line to indicate the certainty of your salvation:

0% _____100%

The Bible teaches, in Hebrews 10:10, that "once saved, always saved." If you were genuine in your original commitment to Jesus Christ as Savior and Lord, must you ask Jesus into your life again?

____Yes ____No (If you *were* genuine in your salvation decision, whom are you doubting?)

Notes

B: BIBLE

The Bible is God's Word. It is inspired (breathed out by God), inerrant (without error) scripture (2 Timothy 3:16; 2 Peter 1:19–21). It is God's message to man. The purpose of this study is to answer two questions about God's Word, the Bible.

1. Throughout scripture, the Bible describes itself. What terms does God use to describe the Bible? From the following non-exhaustive list, look up each passage in your Bible. In first space provided, give the word God used to describe His Word. In the second space provided, apply the word to your life. (Example: John 17:17; God's Word is Truth; God's Word can always be trusted in every circumstance of life.)

Text/Passage	Word(s) for God's Word	Application of the "Word" for God's Word
Exodus 20:1–17 with		
Deuteronomy 6:6–25		
Psalm 19:7–14		
Psalm 119:1		
Psalm 119:1		
Psalm 119:2		
Psalm 119:4		
Psalm 119:5		
Psalm 119:6		
Psalm 119:7		
Psalm 119:9, 11		
Psalm 119:105		
Isaiah 55:10–11		
Jeremiah 20:9		
Jeremiah 23:29		

Luke 8:11

John 17:17

Romans 3:2

Ephesians 5:26

Ephesians 6:17

2 Timothy 3:16–17

Hebrews 5:14

James 1:23

1 Peter 2:2

2 Peter 1:19–21

2.　The theme of the Bible is the King and His kingdom (Daniel 7:27). Jesus Christ is the King (Revelation 17:14). All created things—including believers—are Christ's kingdom (Romans 11:36). How is the Bible organized? Answer the following questions concerning the organization of the Bible:

What are the two general divisions of the Bible?

The _____ Testament (thirty-nine books)

The _____ Testament (twenty-seven books)

What divisions does the Old Testament include?

Books of the _____ (Genesis–Deuteronomy)

Books of _____ (Joshua–Esther)

Books of _____ (Job–Song of Solomon)

The _____ _____ (Isaiah–Daniel)

The _____ _____ (Hosea–Malachi)

What divisions does the New Testament include?

The _____ (Matthew–John),

A book of _____ (Acts)

_____ (Romans–Jude)

A book of _____ (Revelation)

3. Each Bible book has a key verse, a human author, an approximate date it was written, and a theme. Please review the information contained in the following chart on the books of the Bible. Then memorize the names of the books of the Bible, in sequential order.

Bible Book	Key Verse(s)	Human Author(s)	Date Written (approximate)	Theme
Genesis	1:1	Moses	1445–1405 BC	First Things
Exodus	3:8	Moses	1445–1405BC	Freedom
Leviticus	20:78	Moses	1445–1405 BC	Laws
Numbers	14:22–30	Moses	1445–1405 BC	Wandering
Deuteronomy	10:12–13	Moses	1445–1405 BC	Second Law
Joshua	1:29; 11:23	Joshua	1390 BC	Victory
Judges	2:16–19	Samuel	1043–1004 BC	Deliverance
Ruth	4:10–14	Samuel?	987 BC	Redemption
1 Samuel	16:13–14	Samuel, Nathan	931–722 BC	History
2 Samue	17:8–16	Anonymous	931–722 BC	God's Kingdom
1 Kings	9:45	Jeremiah?	646–570 BC	Spiritual Decline
2 Kings	23:27	Jeremiah?	646–570 BC	Two Kingdoms
1 Chronicles	17:11–14	Ezra?	450–430 BC	History
2 Chronicles	5:12	Ezra?	450–430 BC	Two Kingdoms

Ezra	1:3	Ezra	457–444 BC	God's Temple
Nehemiah	4:6	Nehemiah	440 BC	God's City
Esther	4:14–16	Esther?	464 B.C	Providence
Job	37:23–24	Job	1520 BC	Patience
Psalms	150:6	David; Others	1405–430 BC	Praise
Proverbs	1:5–7	Solomon, Others	931–700 BC	Wisdom
Ecclesiastes	1:12–14	Solomon	940 BC	Life's Meaning
Song of Solomon	2:16; 8:7	Solomon	965 BC	Love
Isaiah	61:13	Isaiah	739 BC	Comfort
Jeremiah	7:23–24	Jeremiah	627 BC	Judgment
Lamentations	2:11	Jeremiah	586 BC	Sorrow
Ezekiel	36:24–28	Ezekiel	593 BC	Future Things
Daniel	7:13–14	Daniel	605 BC	Prophecy
Hosea	14:4	Hosea	760 BC	Faithfulness
Joel	2:28–31	Joel	835 BC	Lord's Return
Amos	4:11–12	Amos	760 BC	Judgment
Obadiah	10	Obadiah	845 BC	Judgment
Jonah	4:2	Jonah	782 BC	Obedience
Micah	1:5–9	Micah	735 BC	Society's Sins
Nahum	3:5–7	Nahum	650 BC	Apostasy
Habakkuk	2:4	Habakkuk	609 BC	Faith in God
Zephaniah	1:14–15	Zephaniah	640 BC	Day of the Lord

Haggai	1:14	Haggai	530 BC	Temple
Zechariah	8:23	Zechariah	520 BC	Revival
Malachi	2:17–3:1	Malachi	433 BC	Sin's Curse
Matthew	27:37	Matthew	58–68 AD	Jesus as King
Mark	10:42–47	Mark	55–60 AD	Jesus as Servant
Luke	19:10	Luke	68 AD	Jesus as Man
John	20:30–31	John	90 AD	Jesus as God
Acts	1:8	Luke	68 AD	Church History
Romans	1:16–17	Paul	57 AD	Salvation
1 Corinthians	13:1	Paul	56 AD	The Church
2 Corinthians	5:18–19	Paul	56 AD	Autobiography
Galatians	5:1	Paul	49 AD	Spiritual Liberty
Ephesians	1:20–22	Paul	60 AD	Christ's Body
Philippians	4:4	Paul	60 AD	Joy
Colossians	1:17–19	Paul	60 AD	Authority
1 Thessalonians	1:9–10	Paul	51 AD	Encouragement
2 Thessalonians	2:23	Paul	51 AD	Day of the Lord
1 Timothy	6:11–12	Paul	62 AD	Leadership
2 Timothy	3:14–15	Paul-	67 AD	Last Words
Titus	1:5	Paul	63 AD	Faithfulness
Philemon	17–18 Paul	60	AD	Forgiveness
Hebrews	4:14–16	Unknown	68 AD	Christ Is Best
James	2:14–17	James	49 AD	Practical Faith

1 Peter	4:12–13	Peter	64 AD	Trials
2 Peter	3:3	Peter	65 AD	God's Truth
1 John	5:11–13	John	90 AD	Assurance
2 John	9	John	90 AD	Holiness
3 John	4	John	90 AD	Separated Living
Jude	3	Jude	80 AD	Apostasy
Revelation	1:1	John	95 AD	Future Things

4.   For further study, here are some terms to know when studying God's Word:

Bible:	"Bible" is from a Greek word that means "book" (Matthew 1:1; Luke 4:17).
Revelation:	God's general and specific disclosures to humanity (through creation and His written Word).
Inspiration:	Literally means "God-breathed" (2 Timothy 3:16). It is the way God gave the scriptures.
Inerrancy:	The Bible is without error, in its original manuscripts (2 Peter 1:19–21).
Illumination:	The Holy Spirit's work that allows believers to understand scripture (1 Corinthians 2:11–16).
Infallibility	The Bible is always trustworthy, reliable, and incapable of error (2 Peter 1:19).
Sufficiency	The Bible is always adequate for every situation in life (Psalm 19:7–9).

A CHART OF THE DISPENSATIONS

You have heard of the dispensation of God's grace.
—Ephesians 3:2

Special note: A dispensational outline of the Bible is based on stewardships (time periods). In each, God gave humankind a specific responsibility/commandment to obey. An obedient response results in blessing. A disobedient response results in judgment. Although aspects of previous dispensations can be applied to modern times, the current dispensation is called the Church Age (the Age of Grace).

Dispensation	Responsibility	Response	Results
Innocence Genesis 1:1–3:24	Do not eat of the tree of knowledge Genesis 2:17	Adam and Eve ate of the tree Genesis 3:6	The curses on creation including death Genesis 3:14–19
Conscience Genesis 4:1–8:19	Do what is good and not what is evil Genesis 4:7	Humans did what is evil Genesis 4; 6:5	The flood of Noah Genesis 6:7; 7:10
Human government Genesis 8:20–11:9	Scatter Genesis 9:1–7	Humankind gathered Genesis 11:4	God scattered humankind Genesis 11:7–8
Promise Genesis 11:10–Exodus 19:2	Take God at his word (believe in God) Genesis 12:1–3	Humankind did not take God at His word (doubted His promises) Genesis 13–50	Egyptian bondage Exodus 1–2
Law Exodus 19:3–Acts 2:4	Obey God's Word Exodus 20	Humankind disobeyed God's Word Exodus 32:4	Captivities, judgments, and sufferings Acts 7

Church/Grace Acts 2:4– Revelation 4:1	Receive Jesus Christ as Savior Romans 10:9–10	Humankind rejected Jesus Christ as Savior John 1:10	Eternal condemnation in hell Hebrews 9:27
Millennium Revelation 19:11–22:21	Worship Christ the King Isaiah 66:23	Humans refuses to worship Christ Zechariah 14:16–17	The final judgments Revelation 20:11–15

A CHART ON THE COVENANTS
The words of the covenant …
—Jeremiah 34:18

Special note: A covenant is an agreement between two parties. Throughout scripture, God made agreements between Himself and man. Some of the agreements were conditional, such as man has a responsibility to obey or be punished. Other covenants are unconditional, such as a man has the privileges while God has the responsibility to keep the covenantal agreement. A shortened version of the covenants includes two: innocence/works and grace.

Covenant	Provisions	Provisions	Provisions
Edenic Genesis 2:16–17	Humans have dominion over the earth	Be fruitful and multiply	Do not eat of the tree of knowledge
Adamic Genesis 3:14–19	Sin and sorrow	A Savior will come	Sin's corruptions
Noahic Genesis 9:1–7	Governmental authority	The promise of no more worldwide flood	
Abrahamic Genesis 12:1–3	The promise to Abraham of a land, seed, and blessing	Spiritual and national blessings	
Mosaic Exodus 19:5–6	Spiritual Exodus 20:1–26	Social Exodus 21:1–24:11	Sacrificial Exodus 25–Leviticus 1
Palestinian Deuteronomy 30:1–10	Judgment for disobedience	Blessings for obedience	
Davidic 2 Samuel 7:10–17	A place, peace, and people called Israel	A Savior Jesus Christ	Judgments on Israel's enemies
New (OT) Jeremiah 31:31–33	The Lord's Law	Love	Loyalty
New (NT) Matthew 26:26–28	The body of Jesus	The blood of Jesus	

C: CHURCH

A church is a called-out assembly of born-again believers meeting together to observe the ordinances and worship Jesus Christ. Churches which follow the New Testament model have officers (pastors and deacons). The purpose of this study is to answer three questions about God's true church.

1.   How does God describe His true church?

Matthew 16:18	The church is a "called-out" assembly described by Christ as His _____.
Acts 20:28	The church is a _____ led by the Good, Great, and Chief Shepherd Jesus Christ.
1 Corinthians 3:6–9	The church is a _____ planted by God.
2 Corinthians 11:2	The church is a chaste _____ loved by Christ.
Ephesians 1:18	The church is an _____given to God the Father.
Ephesians 2:15	The church is a new _____ identified with Jesus.
Ephesians 2:19	The church is a holy _____ built by God.
Colossians 1:18–19	The church is a _____ united by God's Holy Spirit.
1 Timothy 3:15	The church is a _____ respecting the Father.
1 Peter 2:9	The church is a royal _____ honoring God.
Revelation 21:9–11	The church is a _____married to Jesus Christ.

Special note: Jesus Christ wants a response of love, respect, worship, and obedience from His church. He wants His church to honor Him. Is Christ preeminent in the local church? Does His church give Christ what He desires?

2.   Using the following list as a guide, answer this question: for what was the early church known?

Acts 1:8 with Isaiah 11:9	The church exists to _____ the lost.
2 Timothy 2:1–2	The church exists to _____ new believers.
Psalm 29:2	The church exists to _____ Jesus Christ as God.
Hebrews 10:25	The church exists to have _____ with the saints.
Ephesians 4:11–13	The church exists to _____ Jesus Christ.
1 Corinthians 16:1–2	The church exists to _____ by returning tangible gifts to God.
Acts 13:1–2	The church exists to participate in local and global _____.
Philippians 4:6–7	The church exists to _____.
Galatians 6:10	The church exists to provide mutual _____.

3.   The Bible reveals the organization of Christ's church. In the spirit of doing all things "decently and in order" (1 Corinthians 14:40), what follows is a sample chart of the organization of the church. Is it yours?

Christ
Pastor
Deacons
Committees
Congregation
Congregation
Committees
Deacons
Pastor
Christ

Don't just *go* to church or *do* church. *Be* the church!

D: DOCTRINE

Believers need mentors. One of the best was Paul, who wrote these encouraging words to a friend in need of direction: "Speak thou the things which become sound doctrine" (Titus 2:1). "Doctrine" is a set of beliefs, a tenet, or a teaching. The purpose of this study is to define the ten major doctrines of scripture, apply them, and then provide a more in-depth study of the doctrine of God.

1.   What are the ten major doctrines of the Bible? Fill in the blank.

Theology proper is the study of _____ (Deuteronomy 6:4–5).

Bibliology is the study of the _____ (2 Timothy 3:16–17).

Christology is the study of the person and work of _____ _____ (Colossians 1:15–17).

Pneumatology is the study of the person and work of the _____ (John 16:13–14).

Anthropology is the study of _____ (Genesis 1:27).

Hamartiology is the study of _____ (Romans 3:23).

Soteriology is the study of _____ (John 3:16).

Ecclesiology is the study of the _____ (Matthew 16:18).

Angelology is the study of _____ (Hebrews 1:14).

Eschatology is the study of _____ _____ (Isaiah 41:22).

2.   Use the following statements to apply the ten major doctrines to your life. Place an X in the appropriate space provided.

I acknowledge that the God of the Bible is the one, true God and that He cares for me.

_____Agree _____ Disagree _____ Not Sure

I believe that the Bible is God's Word and has value in my life.

_____Agree _____ Disagree _____ Not Sure

I believe that Jesus Christ is God and came in human flesh to save my soul from sin.

_____Agree _____ Disagree _____ Not Sure

I believe that the Holy Spirit is God and works within my life to draw me closer to Jesus.

_____ Agree _____ Disagree _____ Not Sure

I believe that the same God Who created the universe can correct the problem of sin.

_____Agree _____ Disagree _____ Not Sure

I believe that all who receive Jesus Christ for salvation are guaranteed eternal forgiveness of sins.

_____ Agree _____ Disagree _____ Not Sure

I believe that God established His local church to proclaim His truths and make disciples.

_____ Agree _____ Disagree _____ Not Sure

I believe that God's "good" angels are "ministering spirits" and can benefit believers.

_____ Agree _____ Disagree _____ Not Sure

I believe that Christ's Second Coming is a source of motivation for godly living.

_____ Agree _____ Disagree _____ Not Sure

If any lines are marked "disagree" or "not sure," please take the time to discuss those biblical doctrines with your presenter. Additional (more specific) applications of each doctrine are the direct result of regular Bible study, scripture meditation, the memorization of God's Word, prayer, and "the working out of what Christ works in." To enhance your learning, find a Bible teacher and church that "rightly divide the Word of Truth" (2 Timothy 2:15). In doing so, you can establish a personal "belief dynamic" and life (style) that is consistent with God's Word.

3. What can the believer know about God? God is called by many names. Each of God's names summarizes a different aspect of His Being. When praying, the believer can address God by the name that best addresses the individual need. (For example, when praying about financial or material needs, the believer can address God as "Jehovah Jireh," the God who meets our needs.) The following are some names of God found in God's Word. (See the chart at the end of this chapter; this is a non-exhaustive list.)

On the appropriate line(s), fill in the description of the name listed. (See the chart at the end of this topic's study).

Elohim (Genesis 3:5; 5:24). God is the _____ and _____ One.

Jehovah (Exodus 3:13–14). God is the _____-_____Holy One to whom believers give _____.

Adonai (Genesis 15:1–7). God is the Lord and sovereign _____ of every believer's life.

El Elyon (Genesis 14:20). God is the God _____ _____.

El Shaddai (Genesis 17:1–3). God is the _____-_____ One who is our source of security.

Jehovah Sabaoth (1 Samuel 17:42–45). He is the Lord of _____, _____, and _____.

El Roi (Genesis 16:13; Psalm 33:13–14). God is the God who _____.

Jehovah Rapha (Jeremiah 8:22). God is the Lord who _____.

Jehovah Nissi (Exodus 17:15). God is the Lord my _____.

Jehovah Mekoddishkem (Exodus 31:13). God is the Lord who _____.

Jehovah Raah (Psalm 23:1). God is the Lord who is my _____.

Jehovah Tsidkenu (Jeremiah 23:6), God is the Lord our _____.

Jehovah Shammah (Ezekiel 48:35). God is the God who is _____.

Jehovah Shalom (Judges 6:22–24). God is the God who is my _____.

El Olam (Genesis 21:10, 22–23). God is the _____ God.

THE NAMES OF GOD

The Lord is His name.

—Exodus 15:3

Special note: Although "the Lord our God is one Lord" (Deuteronomy 6:4), He goes by many names. When the believer gets to know God by name, he gets to know God.

Elohim	Jehovah	Adonai	El Elyon	El Shaddai	Jehovah Sabaoth	El Roi	Jehovah Jireh
The Strong and Faithful One	The self-existent Holy One	The Lord and Master of my life	The God Most High	The All-Sufficient One	The Lord of Hosts	The God who sees	The God who pro-vides
When people let you down	When you need accountability	When you have difficulty submitting your will to God	When you need direction and a point of reference for your life	When you need security, companionship, or the protection of a friend	When you need someone to fight your battles	When you think you are alone	When you have financial needs

Jehovah Rapha	Jehovah Nissi	Jehovah Mekoddishkem	Jehovah Raah	Jehovah Tsidkenu	Jehovah Shammah	Jehovah Shalom	El Olam
The God who heals	The Lord, my banner	The Lord who sanctifies	The Lord who is my Shepherd	The Lord, our righteousness	The God who is there	The God who is my peace	The Ever-lasting God
When you have physical needs or need God's care	When you think you are fighting the battle alone	When you want to be set apart for worship	When you need the love of One who cares	When you need justice or correction	When you feel abandoned by family or friends	When troubled and anxious	When in need of consistency, stability, or a Friend

E: EVANGELISM

While the earth remains, (there is) seedtime and harvest.
—Genesis 8:22

When Paul entered Derbe on his first missionary journey, the Bible describes the steps he took to establish a ministry in that city. He "preached the gospel" (he evangelized the lost, Acts 14:21), he "taught many" (he discipled the converts, Acts 14:21), he "(confirmed) the souls of the disciples" (he equipped believers for service, Acts 14:22), he "(exhorted) them to continue in the faith" (he encouraged the saints, Acts 14:22), they "ordained them elders in every church" (they trained and enlisted leaders, Acts 14:23), and they "commended them to the Lord" (they entrusted the disciples to God, Acts 14:23). The first priority in Derbe was evangelism. Conversions require evangelism. Discipleship ministries and church plants cannot begin without fruit from evangelism.

What does the Bible teach on evangelism? What methods can believers use to evangelize the lost? What ministries can churches initiate to fulfill the Great Commission? The purpose of this study is to answer three questions.

1.   What do the following Bible passages teach on evangelism?

Old Testament Text/Passage	Explanation of the Text
Genesis 8:22	
Psalm 2:8	
Psalm 71:24	
Isaiah 11:9	
Matthew 28:19	
Mark 16:15	
Luke 24:47–48	
John 20:21	
Acts 1:8	

Acts 20:20

Romans 10:15, 17

2 Timothy 4:5

Other:

2.   Respond to the following quotations about evangelism:

The difference between catching men and catching fish: you catch fish that are alive and they die, but you catch men that are dead and they are brought to life.[5]

The world will not be Christianized but should be evangelized.[6]

What can we do on earth that we cannot do in heaven? Evangelize![7]

Our world won't (sic) care how much we know until they know how much we care.[8]

You cannot enjoy the harvest without first laboring in the field.[9]

The good news of the gospel is only good news if it reaches the lost in time.[10]

Evangelism is one beggar telling another beggar where to find bread.[11]

Life, lip, and love are all involved in evangelism.[12]

The world is at your doorstep. Your citizenship in heaven makes your entire world a field to evangelize.[13]

Some wish to live within the sound of church or chapel bell;

---

[5] Benjamin R. De Jong, *Uncle Ben's Quote Book* (Grand Rapids, MI: Baker Book House, 1976), 139.
[6] Dennis J. Hester, *The Vance Havner Quote Book* (Grand Rapids, Baker Book House, 1986), 79.
[7] This is a quote from the sermons of Keith D. Pisani.
[8] A popular quotation of unknown origin.
[9] Source unknown.
[10] Source unknown.
[11] Source unknown.
[12] Original source unknown.
[13] From sermons by Keith D. Pisani.

I want to run rescue shop within a yard of Hell.[14]

The conversion of a soul is the miracle of a moment, but the growth of a saint is the task of a lifetime.[15]

3. What additional quotations do you have concerning evangelism?

4. From John 4:17–30, describe the method Jesus Christ used to reach the lost of His society. Apply Christ's method to your ministry.

Jesus established a point of _____ (John 4:7–9).

Discussion:

Jesus engaged in _____ (John 4:10–14).

Discussion:

Jesus allowed the woman to express _____ (John 4:15).

Discussion:

Jesus exposed the sins of the woman through _____
(John 4:16–19).

Discussion:

Jesus refused to be sidetracked by _____ issues (John 4:20–24).

Discussion:

Jesus brought the woman to a point of _____ (John 4:25–30).

Discussion:

---

[14] A quotation by C. T. Studd of unknown origin.

[15] A quotation combining evangelism and discipleship into one text. Source unknown.

5.   When seeking to win the lost, the Holy Spirit uses God's Word. Specific Bible passages
        can be used with each phase of the evangelistic process. Some passages are as follows.
        (To help in effective evangelism, memorize as many of these passages as possible. If
        possible, have a Bible available and physically show the person the passages in the
        scriptures.)

All have sinned.	(Romans 3:10, 23; Isaiah 64:6; Jeremiah 17:9; Isaiah 53:6; 1 John 1:10; James 2:10).
There is a penalty for sin.	(Ezekiel 18:5; Romans 6:23; Romans 8:6; Luke 13:3, 5; John 3:18, 36).
God sent His Son to save sinners from their sins.	(Romans 6:23; Romans 5:6, 8; 1 Timothy 1:15; John 3:17; Luke 19:10; 1 John 1:7; 1 Peter 3:18; 2 Corinthians 5:21; Isaiah 53:5, 6; John 3:16; 1 John 4:10).
The sinner must receive Jesus Christ as personal Savior to have his sins forgiven.	(Romans 10:9–10; John 1:12; Acts 16:31; Ephesians 2:8–9; John 14:6; Acts 4:12).

        What additional passages can you add to the list?

6.   A variety of methods can be used to lead a person to salvation through faith in
        Jesus Christ. The following presentations are familiar to many involved in evangelistic
        work:

        • *The "ABC's" of Salvation*
        • *The Roman Road*
        • *The Four Spiritual Laws*
        • *Four Things God Wants You to Know*
        • *Tract Evangelism*
        • *Evangelism Explosion*
        • *Sharing Your "Jesus Story" (Orality Evangelistic Method)*
        • *The Bridge to Eternal Life*
        • *Bridge Evangelism (Points of Contact)*
        • *Friendship/Lifestyle Evangelism*
        • *The Way of the Master*
        • *The Wordless Book*
        • Keith D. Pisani's *Salvation! It's Free!* tract
        • *Other Evangelistic Methods*

7.   Discuss the following list of activities that can enhance evangelistic efforts through the local church. The list is coded by category (B = Bible Studies; D = Discipleship Ministries; E = Elderly Ministries; M = Miscellaneous; O = Outreach Ministries; R = Recreational Ministries; S = Seasonal Events; Y = Youth Ministries).

1.	B	Mothers at home Bible study
2.	B	Couples Bible study
3.	B	Men's Bible study
4.	B	Men's breakfast and Bible study
5.	B	Women's Bible study—morning
6.	B	Women's Bible study—evening
7.	B	Women's fellowship(s) with Bible studies
8.	B	Athletes Bible study
9.	B	Home Bible study
10.	D	Discipleship Group Study: Phase 1 (Follow-Up)
11.	D	Discipleship Group Study: Phase 2 (A to Z Bible Study)
12.	D	Discipleship Group Study: Phase 3 (Other Studies)
13.	D	Discipleship—General Study—Sunday school/a.m. service
14.	D	Discipleship One-on-One Study—Sunday morning
15.	D	Discipleship One-on-One Study—weekday(s)
16.	D	Discipleship Small/Cell/Life/Growth/ABF Group(s)
17.	D	Discipleship—Mentoring Group(s)
18.	D	Sunday School/Adult Bible Fellowships
19.	D	.Children's Church/Midweek Children's Groups
20.	E	Senior Saints Outings/Field Trips/Conferences/Retreats
21.	E	Senior Saints Breakfast
22.	E	Senior Saints Craft Time and Bible Study
23.	E	Senior Saints Monthly Fellowship(s)
24.	E	Nursing Home/Assisted Living/Senior Housing Ministries
25.	E	Elderly Day Care
26.	E	"Geezer Leagues" (Softball, Basketball, Tennis, other)
27.	E	Senior Olympiad
28.	E	Senior Lecture Series (Aging, Finances, Diet, Health)
29.	S	Special Holiday Services
30.	S	Christmas: Birthday Party for Jesus
31.	S	Christmas: Cookie Baking in a home or at the church
32.	S	Christmas: Children's Programs
33.	S	Christmas: Gift Wrapping Social
34.	S	Christmas: Neighborhood In-Home Christmas Story
35.	S	Christmas: Gift Exchange/White Elephant/Social
36.	S	Thanksgiving Feast: at Church, in a Restaurant, or at Home

37.	S	Thanksgiving: Homeless/Local Mission Food Distribution
38.	S	Thanksgiving Morning Event (Flag Football, etc.)
39.	S	Halloween: Evangelistic Pumpkin Party
40.	S	Halloween: Trunk or Treat (Children's candy distribution)
41.	S	Halloween: Share tracts while Trick or Treating
42.	S	Fall Festivals/Craft and other event(s)
43.	S	Easter: Cantata/Concert/Musical Event
44.	S	Choir Easter/Christmas Dinner Concert
45.	S	Easter Egg Hunt
46.	S	Good Friday, Sunrise, and Easter Services
47.	S	Memorial Day: Honor the Veterans Day
48.	S	Memorial Day/Labor Day Community Picnic
49.	S	July 4: Honor America Event(s)
50.	S	Valentine's Day: Meal, Auction, or other event(s)
51.	S	Super Bowl Sunday event
52.	S	New Year's Service or All-Nighter
53.	S	Martin Luther King Jr., President's Day, "honor" event(s)
54S	C	hristian Passover Observance
55.	S	Other Holiday Banquets/Feasts of Plenty, etc.
56.	M	Cookbook with gospel message included
57.	M	Special Community Mother's Day Service/Event
58.	M	Special Community Father's Day Service/Event
59.	M	Mother/Daughter Banquet or Event(s)
60.	M	Father/Son or Father/Daughter Event(s)
61.	M	Law Enforcement/Public Workers/Elected Leaders Sunday/Event
62.	M	Graduation Reception at Church
63.	M	Health and Wellness Fairs, Immunization Days, Lecture Series
64.	M	Welcome Committee (Letters, Gifts to new residents)
65.	M	Christian School
66.	M	Christian Preschool
67.	M	Day Care (for children and the elderly)
68.	M	Pulpit Ministry
69.	M	Baptism and Membership Classes
70.	M	Prayer Vigils/All-Night Prayer
71.	M	Concert under the Stars (near the road, outside the church)
72.	M	Specialty Food Event (Pie, BBQ, Chili Cook-Off, etc.)
73.	M	Evangelistic Revival Service(s)
74.	M	Area Crusades

75.	M	Children's Crusades (Keith D. Pisani's book on this topic)
76.	M	Prayer Walk the neighborhood/community
77.	M	Grandparents Camp
78.	M	Day Camp
79.	M	Summer Camp (on campus)
80.	M	Summer Camp (off campus)
81.	M	Science Fair/NASA Camp
82.	M	Provide Music and Other Lessons
83.	M	Adopt a School (Tutoring Ministries, Before and After Care)
84.	M	Tony Evan's *Urban Atlanta Ministries*
85.	M	*Operation Education* (providing teachers/helpers in public schools)
86.	M	Overnight outing (camping/couples' retreats)
87.	M	Concert Series (with guest musicians, etc.)
88.	M	Topical Conference Trips
89.	M	Food Bank
90.	M	Clothes Closet
91.	M	Free Medical Clinic
92.	M	Website/Social Media Evangelism
93.	M	Businessman's Luncheon/Bible Study
94.	M	Counseling Ministries
95.	M	Open a Crisis Pregnancy Center
96.	M	Provide Immigration Classes
97.	M	Host an Ethnic/Language Churches Conference
98.	M	Teach "English as a Second Language" Classes
99.	O	Harvest Events (events that attract a crowd)
100.	O	Car Shows
101.	O	Felt Needs Events (connect with the community's needs)
102.	O	Arts and Crafts Show
103.	O	Venison/Wild Game Dinner/Beast Feasts
104.	O	Public School Released Time Classes (*Child Evangelism Fellowship*)
105.	O	Evangelistic Blitz (neighborhood, event, community)
106.	O	Car Race Outing
107.	O	Jail Ministry
108.	O	Church Visitation Nights, Designated Times
109.	O	AWANA or other Children's Clubs
110.	O	Backyard Bible Clubs (JOY Clubs or other)
111.	O	City Mission Outreach Ministry
112.	O	Street Evangelism Ministries/Soap Box Ministries

113.	O	Choir Dinner Concert—Christmas
114.	O	Family Fun Days—in Gymnasium/auditorium/family center
115.	O	Movie/Entertainment Night
116.	O	Family Roller Skating
117.	O	Family Winterfest/Summerfest
118.	O	"Evangelistic Cube" Street Corner/Park Ministry
119.	O	Puppets in a Park
120.	O	Block Party
121.	O	Community Cook-Out
122.	O	Host an Old-Fashioned Revival Meeting/Tent Crusade
123.	O	Community Evangelistic Survey (door to door)
124.	O	Ladies Tea (in home)
125.	O	Outdoor Open-air Evangelism
126.	O	Tract Distribution at Local Malls
127.	O	Word of Life Drama Team/Life Action Singers
128.	O	College Drama Team
129.	O	Concerts at Local Malls
130.	O	Children's Club Pancake Supper
131.	O	"Jesus" Film at the Local Public/Christian School
132.	O	Fire Truck Display
133.	O	Saturday Farm Animal Petting Zoo
134.	O	Skeet Shoot
135.	O	Children's Club Olympiad
136.	O	Community Sunday
137.	O	Business and Government Leaders Sunday
138.	O	Concert Under the Stars
139.	O	Gazebo Community Concert
140.	O	Door-to-Door Community Outreach
141.	O	Vacation Bible School Preview, Petting Zoo, and Parade
142.	O	Vacation Bible School and Children's Crusade
143.	O	Parade Float and Tract Distribution
144.	O	Tract Distribution (Olympic Torch)
145.	O	Tract Distribution (World Games)
146.	O	Tract Distribution (Veterans Games)
147.	O	Water Booth at Local Fair(s)
148.	O	Chaplaincy for Local Professional Teams
149.	O	Food Truck or other Community Party (on church property)
150.	O	Missions Trips
151.	O	Fishing Trip
152.	O	Children's Club Fair

153.	O	Children's Club Open House
154.	O	Servant Evangelism (help with residential/community projects)
155.	O	Disaster Relief
156.	O	Friend Day—with invitations and luncheon
157.	O	Tract Meet (get a group to hand out tracts)
158.	O	Evangelistic Golf Tournament
159.	O	Labor Day Community Picnic
160.	O	Picnic for Unsaved Friends (church members must bring a friend)
161.	O	Radio Spots/Drive Time Devotionals/Ministries/Talk Times
162.	O	Hospital Evangelism
163.	O	Evangelistic Shopping Sprees
164.	O	Evangelism Explosion (EE)
165.	O	New Resident Welcome Wagon/Letters
166.	O	Matthew Party—for unsaved only
167.	O	Block Party for the Neighborhood
168.	O	Pie Party
169.	O	Baptismal Reception
170.	O	NCAA March Madness Party
171.	O	Super Bowl Party
172.	O	Exercise Club
173.	O	Hunting/Bow Club
174.	O	Media Announcements—one-minute sermonettes
175.	O	Businessmen's Luncheon
176.	O	Park Programs—recreation and tracts
177.	O	Grand Opening Tract Distributions
178.	O	Participate in a Planned Community Event (Booth/Kiosk, Etc.)
179.	O	One on One (witnessing)
180.	R	"Upward Basketball" or other sports event(s)
181.	R	"3 on 3" Tournaments
182.	R	Floor Hockey League
183.	R	Basketball League
184.	R	Volleyball League
185R	B	asketball Night
186.	R	Floor Hockey Night
187.	R	Volleyball Night
188.	R	Basketball and Baseball Sports Clinics
189.	R	Church Softball
190.	R	Sports Clinics/Camps/Academies

191.	R	Open the Gym for Local Groups (Exercise Classes, Leagues, etc.)
192.	R	Outdoor Survival Canoe Trips (Canada, etc.)
193.	R	Exercise Gym Evangelism
194.	R	5K Race
195.	R	Teen Evangelistic Basketball/Volleyball/Flag Football Tournament
196.	R	Youth Olympiad
197.	R	Whitewater Rafting/Canoeing/Boating
198.	R	Rock Climbing
199.	R	Camps
200.	Y	Youth Lock-in
201.	Y	Youth Dating Game
202.	Y	Youth Rallies
203.	Y	Camp Seasonal Activities
204.	Y	Teen Youth Group Meetings
205.	Y	Snow Camp/Water Camp, etc.
206.	Y	Haunted House
207.	Y	Teen Car Wash
208.	Y	Teen Puppet Shows
209.	Y	Other Youth Events (Scavenger Hunts, etc.)

Add your own! Examples are below.

210.	M	Flyer Distribution
211.	M	Mission Trips: International
212.	M	Missions Trips: Stateside: VBS for another church
213.	M	Backpacks for Jesus
214.	M	Plant a church
215.	M	Job Fair
216.	O	
217.	O	
218.		
219.		
220.		

The following gospel tract is the *Evangelism Tract* published by Keith D. Pisani.

Instructions: Hard copy the tract onto the desired paper color. Then fold the tract so the title page (picture) is on the front and the "invitation" page is on the back. Then use this tract to lead souls to Jesus Christ.

SALVATION!

IT'S FREE!

WHAT MUST I DO TO BE SAVED?

1. **ADMIT: YOU ARE A SINNER**
   *For all have sinned and come short
   of the glory of God.*
   (Romans 3:23)

The glory of God is the standard you must
meet to enter God's heaven.

ALL HAVE SINNED—YOU HAVE SINNED.

2. **ACKNOWLEDGE: SIN DESERVES
   PUNISHMENT**
   For the wages of sin is death…
   (Romans 6:23a)

Wages are what you earn.
Death is separation.
The result of sin is separation from God—
forever.

ALL DESERVE PUNISHMENT—
YOU DESERVE PUNISHMENT.

3. **ACKNOWLEDGE: JESUS TOOK
   AND EXPERIENCED YOUR
   PUNISHMENT FOR YOU**
   *But God demonstrated His love toward us,
   in that while we were yet sinners,
   Christ died for us.*
   (Romans 5:8)

JESUS DIED FOR SINNERS—
JESUS DIED FOR YOU.

Because of Jesus Christ, you do not
have to be punished!

WHAT MUST I DO TO BE SAVED?

4. **ASK JESUS INTO YOUR LIFE**
   *But as many as received Jesus,
   to them God gave the power (ability)
   to become the children of God—
   to as many as trust in His name.*
   (John 1:12)

Receive Jesus into your life right now!

Prayer:
Dear God, I admit I am a sinner. I deserve punishment. Jesus took my place. I pray to receive Jesus Christ today. I ask Jesus into my life to forgive me of my sins. In Jesus' name I pray.
Amen.

ASSURANCE: I John 5:11-13

Name: _____

Date: _____

F: FILLING AND FRUIT

When a person has Jesus Christ, complete with the indwelling of the Holy Spirit, he has everything he needs for time and for eternity. This study addresses two topics involving the Holy Spirit of God.

1.　　What does it mean to be filled with the Holy Spirit of God? From the following passages of scripture, determine what the Bible says about Holy Spirit filling:

John 21:15–17	Holy Spirit filling means to be _____ of _____.
Romans 6:11–13	Holy Spirit filling means to be totally _____ to the Holy Spirit's_____.
Luke 5:26	Holy Spirit filling means to be totally _____ by God.

2.　　How can a person be filled with God's Holy Spirit? Ephesians and Colossians are companion books written by Paul. Ephesians 5 and Colossians 3 are parallel passages. Both were written to believers who were hungry for spiritual truth. Read Ephesians 5:19–6:9 and Colossians 3:16–4:1. Then compare Ephesians 5:18 with Colossians 3:16. Since the Ephesians and Colossians passages are parallel, with one exception, what is the secret to being filled with God's Spirit?

　　　　It is _____ _____ with scripture.

3.　　What is the evidence of Holy Spirit filling? From the following passages of scripture, identify biblical evidences of Holy Spirit filling:

Ephesians 5:19	Believers who are filled with God's Spirit are _____ and _____ Christians. *Psalms* are songs of _____ which repeat back to God the scriptures. *Hymns* are songs of _____ directed vertically back toward God. *Spiritual songs* are songs of testimony expressing the _____ of spiritual truth.
Ephesians 5:20	Believers who are filled with God's Spirit are _____ Christians.
Ephesians 5:21	Believers who are filled with God's Spirit are _____ Christians.

4.   What is spiritual fruit? Since Paul spoke of spiritual fruit (Galatians 5:22–23), what is fruit? Although the term "fruit" is mentioned fifty-four times in the Bible, fruit is described in two ways. From the following passages, determine the two ways God described spiritual fruit:

John 15:5   Fruit is the _____ of living organisms.

Matthew 7:20   Fruit is something _____.

5.   In scripture, as in life, there is more than one type of fruit. What types of spiritual fruit are described in the following passages? Look up each passage in your Bible. Then explain each passage in the space provided.

Text/Passage   **Explanation of the Text/Evidence of Fruit**

Matthew 3:8

Matthew 7:16–18

John 4:36

Romans 1:13

Hebrews 13:15

Philippians 1:11

Galatians 5:22–23

6.   Specifically, what fruit does God's Holy Spirit produce in the lives of believers? In the space provided, write a description of each of the nine spiritual fruits.

Galatians 5:22   The fruit toward _____ (the fruit of a vertical relationship)

Love (Song of Solomon 8:7)

Joy (John 15:11)

Peace (Isaiah 26:3–4; John 16:33)

Galatians 5:22   The fruit toward _____ (the fruit of a horizontal relationship)

Patience (Romans 5:3)

Gentleness (2 Samuel 22:36)

Goodness (2 Thessalonians 1:11)

Galatians 5:22–23   The fruit toward _____ (the fruit of an internal relationship)

Faith(fulness) (Romans 12:3)

Meekness (Matthew 5:3)

Temperance (1 Corinthians 9:25)

THE FRUIT OF GOD'S SPIRIT

The fruit of God's Spirit is …
—Galatians 5:22–23

Special note: The fruit of God's Spirit is the byproduct of a believer yielded to Jesus Christ and His Word. Believers who are properly connected to the Vine (Jesus) will bear fruit. Which of the following spiritual qualities can the Heavenly Fruit Inspector find in your life?

Fruit	Description	Notes
Love 1 Corinthians 13:4–8; 1 John 4:7–10	Total unconditional commitment no matter what the cost	
Joy John 17:13; Philippians 4:4	Being right and consistent with the revealed standards of God	
Peace John 16:33; Colossians 3:15	Harmony with God and His Word; Inner contentment with God's will	
Long-suffering Ephesians 4:2; James 5:7–8	Patient endurance and the ability to "remain under" for as long as it takes	
Gentleness 2 Samuel 22:36; Colossians 3:12–13	Sympathetic kindness and God's tender hand, working in the life of the believer, to make him more like Jesus	
Goodness Romans 15:14; Ephesians 4:32	Moral and spiritual excellence	
Faithfulness Romans 12:3; 1 Corinthians 4:1–2	Loyal steadfastness—a living trust for God	

Meekness Matthew 5:5; 1 Timothy 6:11	Power under control	
Temperance 1 Corinthians 9:24–27; 2 Peter 1:6	The person under the Spirit's control (keeping oneself in check)	

G: GIFTS OF THE SPIRIT

If the apostle Paul were to write a letter to you or your church, what would he say? Would the letter be encouraging (like his letters to the Thessalonians), instructive (like his letters to the Ephesians and Colossians), or challenging and corrective (like his letters to the Corinthians and Galatians)? In his letter, would Paul mention the use of your spiritual gifts?

What is a spiritual gift? What gifts are available for modern believers? How can believers discover their spiritual gifts? How can believers apply their gifts to the ministry of the Lord? The purpose of this study is to answer four questions on spiritual gifts.

1.　　What is a spiritual gift? Fill in the blanks.

　　　　A spiritual gift is a God-given _____ to serve Jesus Christ in _____ and _____ ways.

2.　　Why did God give gifts?

　　　　God gave gifts for the _____ of the body of Jesus Christ (1 Peter 4:10).

　　　　God gave gifts for the _____ of believers (Romans 1:11–12).

　　　　God gave gifts for the _____ and glory of Jesus Christ (1 Peter 4:10–13).

　　　　God gave gifts for the _____ of the saints (Ephesians 4:11).

　　　　God gave gifts to _____ the unity of his blood-bought church (1 Corinthians7:1–7).

3.　　In what ways are spiritual gifts different from natural talents? In what ways are spiritual gifts different from spiritual fruit?

　　　　Characteristics of Gifts　　　　**Natural Talent**　　　　**Spiritual Fruit**

4.　　What spiritual gifts did God give for believers? Which of the gifts are available for believers (today)? God gave five types of spiritual gifts. List them and describe them.

　　　　_____ gifts (apostle, prophets, evangelists, pastors, and teachers) given to _____ God's saints.

_____ gifts (prophecy, teaching, exhortation, words of wisdom, and words of knowledge) given to _____ God's Word.

_____ gifts (administration, ministering, showing mercy, and faith) given to _____ God's work.

_____ gifts (helps, giving, and hospitality) given to _____ God's people.

_____ gifts (miracles, healings, tongues, interpretation, and special discernment) given to _____ God's authority in first-century times.

5. Believers need to discover their spiritual gift(s). From the following scripture passages, what should you do to discover your spiritual gift(s)?

    _____ yourself to God as a living sacrifice (Romans 12:1–2).

    _____ for guidance in determining your spiritual gifts (James 1:5).

    _____ the gift(s) God gives (1 Corinthians 12:11).

    _____ your heart's desire concerning your individual gift (Psalm 37:4).

    _____ what gifts others see in you (Acts 6:3–4).

    _____ with your whole heart in your present situation (1 Chronicles 28:9).

    _____ and refine your spiritual gift (1 Peter 4:10–11).

    What have you done to discover your spiritual gift?

6. How can believers apply their gift(s) to the ministry of the Lord? To help identify your spiritual gift(s), participate in the following exercise. (The only gifts listed are gifts available for today.)

    Helps - a God-given ability to serve and help others
            (Romans 12:7; 1 Corinthians 12:28)

    Do you have this gift?_____Yes _____No
    In what ways can you use this gift?

    1. _____

2. _____
3. _____

Teaching - a God-given ability to explain the truths of God
          (Romans 12:7; Ephesians 4:11; 1 Corinthians 12:28)

Do you have this gift?_____Yes_____No
In what ways can you use this gift?

     1. _____
     2. _____
     3. _____

Exhortation - a God-given ability to encourage and motivate others
          (Romans 12:8)

Do you have this gift?_____Yes_____No
In what ways can you use this gift?

     1. _____
     2. _____
     3. _____

Giving - a God-given ability to sacrificially share resources
          (Romans 12:8)

Do you have this gift?_____Yes_____No
In what ways can you use this gift?

     1. _____
     2. _____
     3. _____

Ruling/Governments - a God-given ability to administrate and manage a stewardship
          (Romans 12:8; 1 Corinthians 12:28)

Do you have this gift?_____Yes_____No
In what ways can you use this gift?

     1. _____
     2. _____
     3. _____

Mercy - a God-given ability to sympathize with the needy and comfort the hurting
        (Romans 12:8)

Do you have this gift?_____Yes_____No
In what ways can you use this gift?

1. _____
2. _____
3. _____

Evangelism - a God-given ability to lead souls to Jesus Christ
        (Ephesians 4:11)

Do you have this gift?_____Yes_____No
In what ways can you use this gift?

1. _____
2. _____
3. _____

Pastor/Teacher - a God-given ability to shepherd the flock of God
        (Ephesians 4:11)

Do you have this gift?_____Yes_____No
In what ways can you use this gift?

1. _____
2. _____
3. _____

Faith - a God-given ability to trust God to answer prayer and supply needs (1
Corinthians 12:18)

Do you have this gift?_____Yes_____No
In what ways can you use this gift?

1. _____
2. _____
3. _____

7.   From the results obtained from the just completed exercise, what gift(s) do you have presently?

     1. _____

     2. _____

     3. _____

8.   What additional gift(s) would you like to have?

     1. _____

     2. _____

     3. _____

THE GIFTS OF THE SPIRIT

As every man has received the gift, even so minister [the gift] …

—1 Peter 4:10

Special note: Spiritual gifts are given to believers for use in the context of the local church. Using the chart, determine your spiritual gift and apply it, in service, for Christ.

Gift	Description	Application
HelpsRomans 12:7	A God-given ability to serve and help others	Assisting others
TeachingRomans 12:7	A God-given ability to explain the truths of God	Bible studies and classes
ExhortationRomans 12:8	A God-given ability to encourage/motivate others	Counseling and discipleship
GivingRomans 12:8	A God-given ability to sacrificially share resources	Giving of self and substance to the Lord for regular and special projects
AdministrationRomans 12:8	A God-given ability to administrate and manage a stewardship	Helping in areas of organizationand leadership
MercyRomans 12:8	A God-given ability to sympathize with the needy and comfort the hurting	Actions of kindness
EvangelismEphesians 4:11	A God-given ability to lead souls to Jesus Christ	Soul winning evangelistic endeavors, including witnessing
Pastor/teacherEphesians 4:11	A God-given ability to shepherd the flock of God	Respond to God's call into ministry and then fulfill that call
Faith1 Corinthians 12:18	A God-given ability to trust God to answer prayer and supply needs	Trusting in God's promises through prayer

H: HEAVEN AND HELL

Society has many opinions on heaven and hell. Only God tells the truth. The purpose of this study is to describe the two destinations available to all people. One is heaven. The other is hell. The purpose of this study is to describe the two eternal destinations mentioned in scripture.

1.   Heaven is the place people go who know Jesus Christ as Savior. From the following passages, what is heaven like? Look up each Bible passage. From each passage, describe heaven.

It is _____ (John 14:2).

It is a _____ _____ (Revelation 21:1–3, 10).

It is a _____ place (Revelation 14:13).

It is a place of _____ 1 Corinthians 13:12).

It is the place where believers will _____ again (1 Thessalonians 4:13–17).

It is a place of eternal _____ (Psalm 16:11).

It is a place of _____ and _____ (2 Corinthians 5:10–11

It is a place of _____ to the Savior (Revelation 22:3).

It is a place of indescribable _____ (Revelation 21:10–21).

It is the place of God's eternal _____ (Psalm 11:4).

It is a place of _____ and _____ (Revelation 4–5).

It is a place of _____ (2 Corinthians 5:17; 1 John 3:2).

It is a place for _____ only (John 3:3, 7).

2.   Hell is the place people go who do not know Jesus Christ as Savior. What is hell like? The Bible describes hell. Using your Bible, look up the following verses and write a description of hell:

Psalm 11:6It is a horrible _____.

Psalm 18:5It is a place of _____.

Proverbs 30:16It is a place where the souls of its residents are the "never exhausted" _____ for its fire.

Isaiah 33:14It is a devouring _____.

Matthew 12:37It is a place of no second chances where people can _____.

Matthew 13:42It is a place of spiritual _____.

Matthew 14:11It is a place of total _____.

Matthew 25:41It is the place the _____ and his demons live.

2 Thessalonians 1:9It is a place of everlasting _____.

Hebrews 6:2It is a place of _____.

Revelation 16:10 It is a place of self-inflicted, excruciating _____.

Revelation 20:1It is a _____ pit with no end.

Revelation 20:15It is a _____ of _____ that burns forever.

Revelation 22:10–11It is a place of _____.

3.   Where will you spend eternity: in heaven or in hell?

I: INTEGRITY

Integrity is a public reputation of positive credibility, a lifestyle that is so complete that it is honest even when no One but God is looking, and the opposite of hypocrisy. Do you have integrity?

1.   Introductory exercise: The Bible was written in terms of people. From the following passages, determine which people had integrity and which people needed improvement. Then compare the situations and choices in your life to the lives of the people described in scripture.

Text/Passage	Individual(s)	Demonstrated Integrity?	Consequence
Genesis 3:1–5			
Genesis 3:6			
Genesis 9:22			
Genesis 12:10–20			
Genesis 15:4–5; 16:1–16			
Genesis 27:1–41			
Genesis 39:1–20; 45:4–7			
Exodus 32:1–6			
Numbers 13:26–33			
Numbers 13:36; 14:6–9			
Numbers 23–24			
Joshua 2			
Joshua 7			
Judges 16:4–31			

1 Samuel 17

2 Samuel 11:1–12, 18,

1 Kings 11:1–13

1 Kings 18:25–46

Jonah 1

Matthew 26:48–49

Luke 19:1–9

Acts 5:1–11

2 Corinthians 4:1–6

Revelation 19:11–16

2.　　Two types of integrity are seen in scripture: personal integrity and group integrity. From Daniel 1 and Daniel 6, what factors existed in Daniel's life that allowed him to practice integrity?

Daniel had a close _____ with the Lord (Daniel 1:6; Hebrews 11:33).

Daniel practiced the _____ of his convictions (Daniel 6:10–11).

3.　　From Daniel 3, share insights concerning group integrity.

Group integrity is _____ (Daniel 3:1–7).

Group integrity _____ the test (Daniel 3:8–30).

4.　　Describe an integrity challenge that you faced recently. How did you respond?

5.　　What risks are associated with being a Christian in a non-Christian world? (Examples may include loss of friends, financial hardship, potential job loss, and others.) How does biblical integrity keep believers from submitting to the pressures of society to compromise personal faith?

6.　　Since people are known by the crowd they keep, how has your peer group impacted the quality of your integrity (1 Corinthians 15:33)?

7.　　Read the following passages, then match each passage to the corresponding truth(s):

Passage		Truth	
1 Kings 9:4–5	_____	A.	People of integrity will have their integrity challenged.
Job 2:3	_____	B.	God guards people of integrity.
Job 2:9	_____	C.	God rewards people who show integrity.
Psalm 7:8	_____	D.	Even in the midst of trials, believers can practice integrity.
Psalm 26:8–12	_____	E.	The people who know you most may challenge your integrity.
Proverbs 2:6–8	_____	F.	God can judge according to a person's integrity.
Proverbs 10:9	_____	G.	People of integrity are a blessing to their children.
Proverbs 20:7	_____	H.	Integrity adds stability (security) to a person's life.
1 Timothy 4:12	_____	I.	It is difficult to say something bad about a person with integrity.
Titus 2:7–8	_____	J.	People respect people who practice integrity.

8.　　Read Isaiah 5:18–24. Then apply principles of godly integrity to the following well-known scenarios:[16]

A man has syphilis. His wife has tuberculosis. They had four children. The first child was born blind. The second died soon after childbirth. The third child was born both deaf and dumb. The fourth child acquired tuberculosis. The mother is pregnant with her fifth child, but she is willing to have an abortion if you determine that she should. You will decide for her. Knowing the potential risks, should she have the fifth child, or should she opt for an abortion?

Your answer:

---

[16] These are popular scenarios that I have heard over the years, some of which are included in Joseph F. Fletcher's *Situation Ethics* (Louisville, KY, 1966, 160–169).

(A major university posed this question to a premed class. They voted 100 percent to abort the baby. The professor said, "You have just killed Beethoven.")

A family is being pursued by enemy soldiers. The family is hiding in a house when the soldiers burst into the room where the family is hiding. The youngest child—a baby— starts to cry. The mother kills the baby to prevent the rest of the family from being found. Was the mother right in killing one life to save others?

Your answer:

A man takes out a $1 million life insurance policy to be paid to his family upon his death—regardless of his means of death. The family is impoverished and needs the money. The man becomes infected with a terminal disease. The insurance policy runs out two months before the time of his expected death. If the man kills himself, the family will receive the entire death settlement of $1 million. If the man lives the additional two months, his policy will run out, there is no money to pay the next year's premium, and the family gets nothing. What should the man do: kill himself so his family gets the money or remain alive until God takes him home?

Your answer:

In World War II, a freighter is attacked and sunk one hundred miles from the shore of an island. Thirty sailors find refuge in a lifeboat. The lifeboat is large enough to hold fifteen passengers. There is enough food and water for ten sailors to survive. If twenty sailors throw themselves overboard and drown, the remaining ten sailors can make it to the island and live. If no one throws themselves overboard, everyone will die. What would you do? Why?

Your answer:

A man and his wife visit a foreign country. The political leader in that country is antagonistic to people with the man's ethnic background. Although the leader is attracted to the man's wife, he is not aware that the woman is married to the man. Should the man admit that the woman is his wife, or should he lie about her identity and call the woman his sister, thus saving his own life (Genesis 12:10–20)?

Your answer:

You are a pilot in the military. President Truman has ordered you and your crew to drop an atomic bomb on Hiroshima, Japan. It will spare a potential 1 million American casualties in the upcoming invasion on Japan. On the other hand, it will kill 90,000 Japanese in Hiroshima. Knowing that a court martial awaits those who disobey a presidential command, do you obey the order and drop the bomb to save 1 million Americans, or do you disobey the order to save 90,000 Japanese lives?

Your answer:

(An alternate scenario is that *you* are President Truman. What decision would *you* make if you were the president? Also, be careful how you answer. My father was on a tarmac at an air base in North Carolina, waiting to board a military transport plane that would carry him to Japan, when the bomb was dropped. If not for the bomb, potentially, the author would not be born and this book would not be written.)

Situations are tempting you to place more authority on people's opinions than the revealed Word of God. Emotions are playing havoc with your ability to decide between "a love response" or "a biblical response" that may include love. In the scenarios of your life, when your friends want you to engage in activities that are contrary to the scriptures, do you obey the Bible, or do you rationalize your participation in those behaviors based on the situation(s) involved and/or the temporary advantage participation in those behaviors produces, such as drugs, sex, drinking, smoking, cheating, hiding the truth from a teacher, parents, or employer, stealing from your work, using someone else's paper or identification document, misrepresenting a product, attending places or parties that do not please Jesus Christ, using profanity, engaging in hypocritical behavior to impress another person, compromising biblical convictions because you want to please someone other than God, lying, hiding the truth for the purpose of manipulating a situation or its outcome, and misusing information through gossip or slander? Is truth today still truth tomorrow, or does truth change according to the scenario? How do you respond?

Your answer:

J: JESUS CHRIST

Jesus Christ is God. The purpose of this study is to examine the names and nature of Jesus Christ.

1.   In five words or fewer, who is Jesus Christ to you?

2.   Throughout scripture, Jesus Christ is known by different names. By what names is Jesus called? The following is a list of some biblical names for Jesus. (Look up each reference in scripture, identify the name for Jesus Christ, and identify the name's significance).

Text/Passage	Name	Significance of the Name
Psalm 23:1		
Isaiah 9:6–7		
Isaiah 9:6–7		
Isaiah 9:6–7		
Isaiah 9:6–7		
Isaiah 9:6–7		
Isaiah 53:3		
Matthew 1:21		
John 1:1		
John 1:29		
John 1:34		
John 8:12		
John 14:6		
1 Timothy 1:15		
1 Timothy 2:5		
Titus 3:4_		

Hebrews 3:1

Revelation 1:8

Revelation 1:8

Revelation 19:14

3.   Society sees Jesus in different ways. To some, He is a teacher and moral philosopher. To others, He is one of many prophets. According to scripture, Jesus Christ is God. He does the works of God. He deserves the worship given to God. In what ways does scripture claim Jesus to be God? Look up the following references, and explain God's teachings concerning the deity of Jesus Christ:

Matthew 5:21–22 The _____ of Jesus Christ prove He is God.

John 1:1 The _____ of Jesus Christ prove He is God.

John 1:3, 30 The _____ of Jesus Christ prove He is God.

John 5:23 Creation's _____ of Jesus Christ proves He is God.

John 10:30, 36 The _____ of Jesus Christ prove He is God.

John 16:15 The _____ of Jesus Christ prove He is God.

4.   Because Jesus Christ is God, He existed before His birth. Any time the phrase "the Angel of the Lord" appears in the Old Testament, it is a "pre-Bethlehem" appearance of Jesus Christ. From the following list, how did the pre-incarnate Jesus (pre-Bethlehem Jesus) appear to people before He was born (twenty-nine Old Testament appearances)?

Text/Passage	**Appearance as the Angel of the Lord**
Genesis 16:7	
Genesis 21:17	
Genesis 22:11, 15	
Exodus 3:1–6	
Exodus 14:19	

Exodus 23:20–23

Exodus 32:34

Numbers 22:21–35

Joshua 5:13–15

Judges 6:12

Judges 13:3

1 Kings 19:5, 7

2 Kings 1:3, 15

1 Chronicles 21:12

Isaiah 63:9

Zechariah 1:11, 12

Malachi 3:1

Text/Passage   **Other Old Testament Appearance**

Genesis 3:8

Genesis 4:16

Genesis 17:1

Genesis 18:1

Genesis 48:16

Exodus 3:14, 15

Exodus 13:21

Exodus 19:18, 24

Exodus 33:21–23

Exodus 40:34–38

1 Kings 8:10, 11

2 Chronicles 3:13

5.　　Jesus Christ preached numerous sermons. One of His most famous is the

Sermon on the Mount (Matthew 5–7). The Beatitudes comprise the first part of that sermon. Provide a description of the Beatitudes (Matthew 5:3–12).

- Believers should have a proper attitude toward _____ (Matthew 5:3).
- Believers should have a proper attitude toward _____(Matthew 5:4–6).
- Believers should have a proper attitude toward the _____(Matthew 5:7–9).
- Believers should have a proper attitude toward _____(Matthew 5:10–12).

6.　　From the following passages, what events did Jesus Christ experience during His final "passion week" on earth?

John 12:12–19His _____ _____ into Jerusalem (His presentation).

John 13–16His _____ _____ (foot washing, Communion).

Matthew 26:36–56The _____ of _____ (prayer for the lost, betrayal, arrest).

Matthew 26:57–27:32 His _____ (Peter's betrayals, crown of thorns).

John 19:17–24His _____ on Calvary's cross.

John 20:1–23His _____ from the grave.

7.　　Jesus Christ is the Lord of every believer's life (Philippians 2:5–11; 1 Corinthians 4:4–5). To what degree do you submit the following to the Lordship of Jesus Christ? (Place an X at the appropriate place on each line.)

your relationships (Ephesians 4:1–3)
0%_____100%

your work and chosen vocation (Ephesians 4:4–13)

0%_____100%

the circumstances of your life (Ephesians 4:14–16)

0%_____100%

your thought life (Ephesians 4:17–24)

0%_____100%

your emotions (Ephesians 4:25–29)

0%_____100%

the decisions you make in life (Ephesians 4:30–32)

0%_____100%

your daily walk (Ephesians 5:1–17)

0%_____100%

your heart's control to the Spirit's control (Ephesians 5:18–20)

0%_____100%

your family life (Ephesians 5:21–6:4)

0%_____100%

your job (Ephesians 6:5–9)

0%_____100%

the protection of your heart (Ephesians 6:10–17)

0%_____100%

your prayer life (Ephesians 6:18

0%_____100%

K: KEYS TO SPIRITUAL GROWTH

The last words a person speaks are often the most important. Simon Peter's last words were "Grow in grace, and in the knowledge of our Lord and Savior Jesus Christ. To Him be glory both now and forever. Amen" (2 Peter 3:18). The purpose of this study is to evaluate the believer's personal commitment to growing in Jesus Christ. This study places emphasis on two growth-related topics: growing into maturity and the believer's growth mentality.

1.   God expects believers to grow into maturity. From the following passages, what five stages of spiritual growth does scripture describe?

Believers begin as spiritual _____ (1 Peter 2:2).

Believers continue to grow into _____ (Ephesians 4:14).

Believers continue to grow into _____ (1 John 2:12).

Believers continue to grow into _____ _____ (1 John 2:13).

Believers continue to grow into _____ (1 John 2:14).

2.   2.From the following scripture passages, in what three fields is spiritual growth harvested?

Believers grow in _____ (1 Peter 3:18).

Believers grow in _____ (2 Peter 3:18).

Believers must grow in _____ and _____ (2 Thessalonians 1:3).

3.   Since every believer should grow, how can believers grow?

_____ to doubt your assurance of salvation (1 John 5:11–13).

Publicly _____ your salvation experience to someone close to you. (Romans 10:9–11, 15).

_____ the Bible and _____ (2 Timothy 3:16–17; Philippians 4:6–7).

Faithfully _____ a Bible preaching church (Hebrews 10:25).

Be _____ following your salvation (Acts 2:41).

_____ a Christian fellowship group (1 Corinthians 15:33).

Make _____ the pattern of your life (1 Corinthians 16:1–2).

_____ God's Word to memory (Psalm 119:11).

Be _____ to God and others (Ecclesiastes 4:9–10).

_____ the living Savior (Ephesians 2:10).

4.   God wants believers to develop a growth mentality. From the following scripture passages, identify the areas in which a believer should grow:

2 Peter 1:5 Add to your saving faith _____.

2 Peter 1:5 Add to your virtue _____.

2 Peter 1:6 Add to your knowledge _____.

2 Peter 1:6 Add to your temperance _____.

2 Peter 1:6 Add to your patience _____.

2 Peter 1:7 Add to your godliness _____.

2 Peter 1:7 Add to your brotherly kindness _____.

5.   Chart your spiritual growth.

SEVEN DAYS OF CHRISTIAN GRACE

Add to your faith.

—2 Peter 1:5–7

Special note: Place this chart somewhere you can see it. On each day of every week, live out your faith by demonstrating at least one grace. See the difference it makes in your life.

Day	Grace	Application
Monday	Virtue	Pursue moral excellence and practice clean living.
Tuesday	Knowledge	Know God's Word and act upon it, with discernment.
Wednesday	Temperance	Practice the discipline of self-control.
Thursday	Patience	Develop an ability to endure trials. Then translate your problems into praise.
Friday	Godliness	Be Christlike in your thoughts and actions.
Saturday	Brotherly Kindness	Be a peacemaker and show God's grace to all.
Sunday	Love	Demonstrate your commitment to Christ by being intentional in your acts of love to others.

And beside this, giving all diligence, add to your faith virtue; and to virtue knowledge; And to knowledge temperance; and to temperance patience; and to patience godliness; And to godliness brotherly kindness; and to brotherly kindness charity. (2 Peter 1:5–7)

L: LAST DAYS

Scripture's greatest Prophet unveiled eternal truth when He said, "However, when He, the Spirit of truth, has come, He will guide you into all truth … and He will tell you *things to come*" (John 16:13). The purpose of this study is to review the major events that are yet to take place on God's prophetic calendar.

1.   In Matthew 24–25, Christ gave four signposts that point to end time events. From the following passages of scripture, what signs did Christ reveal?

   Matthew 24:1–3 The rebuilt temple will be _____.

   Matthew 24:4–5 _____ will come.

   Matthew 24:6–8 _____ will happen.

   Matthew 24:27–31 _____ will happen to those who believe.

2.   According to 1 Thessalonians 4:13–17, what is the next event on God's prophetic calendar?

   The _____ of the church.

3.   According to Daniel 9:26–27, what end-time figure will commit an abomination of desolation in Jerusalem's temple during the coming tribulation?

   _____.

4.   From Ezekiel 38–39, Revelation 19, and Revelation 20, describe the three campaigns (battles) of Armageddon.

   Ezekiel 38–39 (midtribulation)

   Revelation 19 (end of tribulation)

   Revelation 20 (end of millennium)

5.   From the following passages of scripture, what happens during the days after the second battle of Armageddon?

   Daniel 12:1–3

   Revelation 19:17–18

Zechariah 13:1–5

Zechariah 14:6–11

2 Peter 3:10–14

6.   God rewards faithfulness in the form of crowns. Of the following crowns, circle the one(s) you anticipate earning to cast at the feet of Jesus (Revelation 4:10):

the Servant's crown1 Corinthians 9:24–27

the Soul-winner's crown1 Thessalonians 2:19

the Sufferer's crownJames 1:12

the Second Coming crown2 Timothy 4:8

the Shepherd's crown1 Peter 5:1–4

7.   Create a timeline (outline) of the book of Revelation. Pray for someone who needs Jesus Christ as Savior.

(The key verse of the Revelation of Jesus Christ is Revelation 1:19, which says, "The things which thou hast seen, the things which are, and the things which shall be thereafter." The theme is Revelation 1:7, "Behold, He cometh." A general outline is as follows:

Christ as _____ of the churches (Revelation 1–3).

Christ as _____ over the nations (Revelation 4–20).

Christ as the _____ of eternity (Revelation 20–21).

8.   Examine the chart at the end of this study. What are the five major judgments found in scripture? In each, who is judged? What is judged? Where is the judgment? Why is the judgment taking place? What lessons can you learn from each judgment?

(See the chart at the end of this chapter.)

GOD'S JUDGMENTS

The soul that sinneth, it shall die.

—Ezekiel 18:5

Special note: For each judgment, answer the corresponding questions and apply the lessons of the judgment(s).

Judgment	Who?	What?	Where?	Why?	Lessons
SinJohn 5:24	Sinners	Sin	Cross	Original Sin	Without the sacrifice of Jesus at Calvary, the sinner is judged for eternity.
Self1 Corinthians 11:32–33	Believers	Unfaithfulness to Jesus	Communion Service (Lord's Table)	God wants to fellowship with faithful followers.	Confession and repentance restore fellowship with God.
Service2 Corinthians 5:10–11	Believers	Unfaithfulness to Jesus Christ	Bema Seat Judgment	God rewards for faithfulness and rebukes unfaithful believers.	The believer's worship, works, and prayer life must be properly motivated to receive rewards.
SocietyJoel 3:13–16	Nations	Rebellion against God and rejection of Jesus	Armageddon	In unbelief, the nations rebel against God.	Receive Christ today or run the risk of being a part of God's judgment at the end of the tribulation
SoulsRevelation 20:11–15	Unbelievers	Unbelief (failure to receive Christ as Savior)	Great White Throne Judgment	Hebrews 9:27:God judges the sin of unbelief.	Everyone lives somewhere for eternity. The difference is how a person responds to the gospel message of Jesus.

THE TRIBULATION JUDGMENTS

The Lamb broke the first seal.

—Revelation 6:1

Special note: Three consecutive phases of judgment are revealed in Revelation 6–19: seal, trumpet, and bowl judgments). All judgments begin after the rapture of the church.

Judgment				
Seal judgments Revelation 6:1–7:3	(1) Antichrist brings peace (Revelation 6:1–2).	(2) War (Revelation 6:3–4)	(3) Famine (Revelation 6:5)	(4) Death (Revelation 6:7–8)
	(5) Persecution (Revelation 6:9)	(6) Destruction (Revelation 6:12–16)	(7) Silence in heaven (Revelation 7:2–3)	
Trumpet judgments Revelation 8:7–11:19	(1) Hail, Fire, and Blood (Revelation 8:7)	(2) Falling Meteor (Revelation 8:8–9)	(3) Falling Star (Revelation 8:10–11)	(4) Sun, Moon, and Stars Darkened (Revelation 8:12)
	(5)Locusts (Revelation9:3–12)	(6) Israel Invaded (Revelation 9:13–21)	(7)Earthquake (Revelation 11:19)	
Vial/Bowl judgmentsRevelation 16:1–21	(1) Boils (Revelation 16:1–2)	(2) Sea of Blood (Revelation 16:3)	(3) Rivers of Blood (Revelation 16:4–7)	(4) Sun Scorches Man (Revelation 16:8–9)
	(5) Darkness (Revelation 16:10–11)	(6) Euphrates Dries Up (Revelation 16:12–16)	(7) Hail (Revelation 16:17–21)	

M: MINISTRIES OF SERVICE

Paul wrote, "We are [His work of art: *poyeema*], created in Christ Jesus unto good works *(erga)*" (Ephesians 2:10). The term translated "good works" is the root for the English word energy. Believers are to put energy into their works and serve Jesus Christ with enthusiasm. The purpose of this study is to examine the words and works associated with serving Jesus Christ. Every believer should serve.

1.   What biblical terms are associated with the believer's ministries of service? Look up the following passages and identify the terms used in scripture for Christian service:

John 15:20 The servant as a _____-_____ *(doulos)*.

Matthew 23:11 The servant as an active _____ *(diakonos)*.

Romans 12:1 The servant as a religious _____ *(latria, latruo)*.

Matthew 12:18 The servant by _____ or as an apprentice *(pais)*.

Hebrews 3:4–5 The servant as a respected _____ *(therapon)*.

1 Peter 2:18 The servant as a _____ of a _____ *(oiketees)*.

2 Timothy 2:3–4 The servant as a _____ in the army of Jesus Christ *(strateuo)*.

1 Corinthians 4:1 The servant as one who is under _____ *(huperetees)*.

2.   From the following scripture passages, who performed works of service unto God?

Exodus 35–38

Leviticus (in the tabernacle)

Nehemiah 3

Matthew 20:28

Acts 13

Romans 16:1

James 1:1–2

3. Every local church has service opportunities. Where do you fit in? How are you serving Jesus Christ? On the following list (keyed to available spiritual gifts), place an X on the appropriate line(s):

Leadership	Currently	As God Leads
Pastor	_____	_____
Church officer	_____	_____
Elected position	_____	_____
Departmental head	_____	_____
Paid or appointed position	_____	_____
Administrative position	_____	_____
Other	_____	_____

Teaching	Currently	As God Leads
Age you prefer:	_____	_____
Sunday school	_____	_____
Children's church	_____	_____
AWANA or other club	_____	_____
Vacation Bible school	_____	_____
Backyard club	_____	_____
Youth work	_____	_____
Bible study	_____	_____
Discipleship: one on one	_____	_____
Discipleship: group	_____	_____
Mentoring	_____	_____
Small groups/life groups	_____	_____
Other	_____	_____

Evangelism	Currently	As God Leads
Witnessing	_____	_____
Visitation	_____	_____
Missions	_____	_____
Hospital, nursing home	_____	_____
Jail ministries, etc.	_____	_____
Evangelistic home studies	_____	_____
Tract distribution	_____	_____
Recreational outreach	_____	_____
Small groups/life groups	_____	_____
Other	_____	_____

Exhortation and Faith	Currently	As God Leads
Prayer ministries	_____	_____
Counseling	_____	_____
Encouragements	_____	_____
Hospitality	_____	_____

Other   _____   _____

Giving	Currently	As God Leads
Tithes and offerings	_____	_____
Special needs	_____	_____
Projects	_____	_____
Missions	_____	_____
Private assistance	_____	_____
Time and talents	_____	_____
Other	_____	_____

Helping	Currently	As God Leads
Building and grounds	_____	_____
Elderly assistance	_____	_____
Office or sound room	_____	_____
Nursery or children	_____	_____
Transportation	_____	_____
Skills	_____	_____
Refreshments	_____	_____
Hospitality	_____	_____
Craft and design skills	_____	_____
Christian school	_____	_____
Other	_____	_____

Worship	Currently	As God Leads
Music	_____	_____
Prayer	_____	_____
Ushering	_____	_____
Preaching/teaching	_____	_____
Attentiveness	_____	_____
Friendliness	_____	_____
Compassion	_____	_____
Unity of Spirit	_____	_____
Fellowship	_____	_____
Other	_____	_____

Mercy	Currently	As God leads
Hospital calling	_____	_____
Prayer	_____	_____
Home visits	_____	_____
Elderly care	_____	_____
Communications of encouragement	_____	_____
Special needs	_____	_____
Clothes closet/food bank	_____	_____
Other	_____	_____

4.   What type of servant are you (place an X where appropriate)?

       Bond-slave (*doulos*) ____ Active ____ Needs Improvement

       Active worker (*diakono*s)____ Active ____ Needs Improvement

       Religious worker (*latria*)____ Active ____ Needs Improvement

       Apprentice/learner (*pais*)____ Active ____ Needs Improvement

       Respected leader (*therapon*)____ Active ____ Needs Improvement

       Household member *(oiketees)*____ Active ____ Needs Improvement

       Soldier of God (*strateuo*)____ Active ____ Needs Improvement

       Under rower (*huperaytos*)____ Active ____ Needs Improvement

5.   In what ways can you improve as a servant (in attitude, activities, etc.)?

6.   Make a list of servants from scripture. In what ways are you like them?

       Servant   Similarities

N: NEW NATURE

Peter wrote,

> Grace and peace be multiplied unto you through the knowledge of God, and of Jesus our Lord, according as His divine power hath given unto us all things that pertain unto life and godliness, through the knowledge of Him that hath called us to glory and virtue: whereby are given unto us exceeding great and precious promised [things]: that by these ye might be partakers of the divine nature, having escaped the corruption that is in the world through lust. (2 Peter 1:2–4)

When a person is regenerated (born again), God purifies his life (1 John 3:3), he makes a clean break with corruption caused by evil desire (2 Peter 1:4), and God imparts His nature into the life of every believer (2 Corinthians 5:17). Scripture calls this divine nature the new man (Colossians 3:10). Theologians label it the new nature.

The purpose of this study is to examine the distinctions between what believers were before they came to Jesus Christ and what believers are in Jesus Christ. It is a contrast between the old and the new.

1. Sinners possess an old nature. From the following passages of scripture, how does God describe the old nature? Look up each passage of scripture and put a descriptive word on the line provided.

    Matthew 26:41   The old nature _____ a person from doing God's will.

    John 1:13   The old nature has a _____ that that is contrary to God's will.

    Romans 3:20   The old nature is comfortable with _____ not regeneration.

    Romans 7:5   The old nature _____ every aspect of a person's life.

    Romans 7:18   The old nature _____ the person to disregard God and His Word.

    Romans 7:25   The old nature _____ its way.

    Romans 8:3–4   The old nature _____ believers spiritually.

    Romans 8:8–9   The old nature _____ itself.

    Romans 8:12–13   The old nature _____ the believer's fellowship with God.

Romans 13:14   The old nature wants a _____ in the believer's life.

1 Corinthians 1:26 The old nature has a _____ that is not wise in God's sight.

1 Corinthians 5:4–5 The old nature _____ fellowship with God and His people.

Galatians 5:13   The old nature _____ its lusts and _____ its appetites.

Galatians 6:8   The old nature _____ what it sows.

Ephesians 2:3   The old nature _____ the presence, existence, and indwelling of God's Holy Spirit.

Philippians 1:21   The old nature becomes its own sphere of _____.

Colossians 2:11–12 The old nature _____ as if the believer is not saved.

2 Peter 2:9–18   The old nature can be _____ when the believer _____ to God's Holy Spirit.

2. At the moment of salvation, believers receive a new nature from God. What does the believer get when he acquires his new nature from God? From the following scripture passages, identify the changes that take place when a believer gets his new nature:

He is given new _____ (John 3:6–7).

He acquires a new _____ (John 1:12).

He receives a new _____ (Ezekiel 36:26).

He responds to new _____ _____ (Ephesians 4:23–24).

He discerns with a new biblical _____ (John 3:3).

He becomes a new _____ (2 Corinthians 5:17).

3. Every believer is confronted with temptations to sin in thought and in action. Examine the following scripture passages, review the list of questions that are popular in many Christians circles, and subject your thoughts and actions to the appropriate questions:

1 Corinthians 10:31	Will God be glorified?
1 Corinthians 6:12	Is it best for me and others?
1 Corinthians 6:12	Will I be controlled by it?
1 Corinthians 10:33	Is this an issue with others?
1 Corinthians 14:26	Will it help me spiritually?
1 Corinthians 14:40	Would it cause confusion?
1 Corinthians 16:14	Is it a loving thing to do?
2 Corinthians 6:3–4	Would it hurt my service for Christ?
Philippians 2:14	Can I be positive about it?
Colossians 3:17	Can I do it for the Lord?
Colossians 3:20	Would people I respect say it is right?
1 Thessalonians 4:13–17	Do I want to be doing it when Jesus comes?
1 Thessalonians 5:17	Have I prayed about it?
1 Thessalonians 5:18	Can I thank God for it?
1 Thessalonians 5:21	Is it of lasting value?
1 Timothy 6:17	Will I look back on this with joy?
2 Timothy 4:5	Is it "of God"?
Titus 2:7	Is it good for others?
Titus 2:10	Does the Bible say it is right?
Hebrews 12:1	Is it a weight?
Hebrews 13:18	Would I have to lie to cover it up?
1 Peter 2:17	Can I respect others who do it?
1 Peter 3:15	Does it impact my testimony for Christ?

4.   Make a list of thoughts, attitudes, and actions. Submit each thought, attitude, and action to the questions listed. (In the list, include some thoughts, attitudes, and actions that may be considered gray areas in life.)

5.   In thirty words or fewer, in what ways has this study changed your thought life? Your attitudes? Your actions?

6.   When confronted by temptations to sin, which responds the most: your sin nature or your new nature?

_____ Sin Nature
_____ New Nature
_____ Not Sure

O: OBEDIENCE

Dr. Robert T. Ketcham was a prominent leader in the mid-twentieth century American church. He said, "I have nothing to give to God, but obedience."[17]Obedience is best understood when it is demonstrated and personified in life.

The purpose of this study is to examine the concept of obedience in terms of three biblical personalities. Since the Bible is a mirror, in the lives of these three biblical personalities, the believer should see something of himself.

1.   Abraham was obedient to God. On what seven promised blessings did Abraham act?

        The blessing of a _____ (Genesis 12:2).

        The blessing of _____ (Genesis 12:2).

        The blessing of _____ (Genesis 12:2).

        The blessing of influential _____ (Genesis 12:2).

        The blessing of _____ (Genesis 12:3).

        The blessing of _____ (Genesis12:3).

        The blessing of the _____ (Genesis 12:3).

2.   Jonah was disobedient. What three steps did Jonah take toward obedience?

        Jonah 1Jonah _____ _____ from God.

        Jonah 2Jonah _____ _____ to God.

        Jonah 3–4Jonah _____ with God.

3.   Simon Peter was both obedient and disobedient. From Luke 5:1–11, Luke 23:53, John 21:15–17, and Acts 3, tell Simon Peter's "obedience" story.

        Luke 5:1–11

        Luke 22:54–62

        John 21:15–17

---

[17] J. Murray Murdoch, *The Portrait of Obedience* (Schaumburg, IL: Regular Baptist Press, 1979), 13.

Acts 3

4.　　Each of the following passages teaches a truth concerning obedience. Look up each passage of scripture. Match each passage to its corresponding truth.

1 Samuel 15:22_____A. Obedient believers gain spiritual strength.

Job 17:9_____B. Believers who love Jesus Christ prove their love through obedience.

Psalm 119:59_____C. Friendship for Jesus Christ is proven through faithful obedience.

Psalm 119:60_____D. Obedience is a thought-out choice.

John 14:21_____E. Obedience from the heart is better that ritualistic sacrifice.

John 14:23_____F. God wants (expects) instant obedience.

John 15:10, 14_____G. Disobedience is sin.

Acts 5:29_____H. Love for Jesus motivates the believer to obey Christ.

2 Thessalonians 3:14_____ I. Believers should obey God's established leaders.

Hebrews 13:17_____J. When God and government disagree, obey God.

James 4:17_____K. Believers are under God's authority to obey His Word.

1 Peter 1:2_____L. Believers are called unto obedience.

5.　　What lessons can you learn from the life of Abraham? Jonah? Simon Peter?

6.　　Test your obedience. As Peter sat around the fire, it is believed that Jesus Christ pointed to his companions, to the fishing boats that represented Peter's career, and to the campfire around which were Peter's possessions. Walk in Peter's sandals. Allow Jesus to confront your life.

Do you love Jesus Christ more than your profession?

　　　　　_____ Yes　　　　　_____ No　　　　　_____ Not Sure

Do you love Jesus Christ more than your possessions?

　　　　　_____ Yes　　　　　_____ No　　　　　_____ Not Sure

Do you love Jesus Christ more than the people with whom you associate?

_____ Yes　　　　　_____ No　　　　　_____ Not Sure

Do you love Jesus Christ more than you love yourself?

_____ Yes　　　　　_____ No　　　　　_____ Not Sure

7.　　Nine of the Old Testament's Ten Commandments are repeated for the church. (Christ's Sunday resurrection changed "Saturday Sabbath keeping" to "first day of the week" worship for the church.) From the following chart, in what ways do you apply God's Ten Commandments to your life (chart)?

THE TEN COMMANDMENTS

And God spoke all these words, saying ...
—Exodus 20:1

Special note: For each commandment, apply the lesson to your life.

First Four Commandments: Relationship to God	Lesson	Last Six Commandments: Relationship to Man	Lesson
No other gods. Exodus 20:3	God must be #1 and the only god in your life.	Honor your father and mother. Exodus 20:12	See parents as God's representatives in the home.
No idols/images. Exodus 20:4–6	There can be no substitutes for God.	Do not murder. Exodus 20:13	Life is sacred, and authority over it belongs to God alone.
Do not use God's name in vain.Exodus 20:7	Remember who God is, and trust in Him in every situation.	Do not commit adultery.Exodus 20:14	Keep yourself from all immorality.
Remember God's holy day.Exodus 20:8–11	Set apart God's day for worship.	Do not steal. Exodus 20:15	There are no shortcuts to prosperity.
		Do not lie. Exodus 20:16	Be honest in all things.
		Do not covet. Exodus 20:17	Be content with what you have.

P: PRAYER

Prayer is the believer's declaration of dependence on God. It is a person's preoccupation with God. It is talking to God. The purpose of this study is to examine the biblical terms for prayer and some selected texts on prayer.

1.   The doctrine of prayer takes a seven-faceted jewel of revelation to reveal its brilliance. List and describe the seven biblical terms for prayer.

   3 John 2   A prayer that expresses a _____ (*ukomai*).

   Philippians 1:9   A prayer that expresses a _____ _____ toward _____ (*prosukomai*).

   Matthew 9:38   A prayer that is a specific _____ based on a need (*deomai*).

   Matthew 7:7   A prayer of _____ from a lesser to a greater (*aiteo*).

   Romans 8:26–27   A prayer of _____ on behalf of others (*entunkano*).

   Hebrews 5:7   A prayer of _____ to ask for protection (*hiketeeria*).

   John 14:16   A prayer of _____ made between _____ (*erotao*).

2.   What are seven needs that believers have in association with prayer? List them, and describe them.

   Matthew 7:7–8   Believers need to _____ God's _____ through prayer.

   Ephesians 3:14   Believers need to _____ God's _____ for prayer.

   Psalm 63:1–4   Believers need to _____ a _____ in prayer.

   Psalm 24:3–5   Believers need to _____ the _____ of prayer.

Luke 11:1   Believers need to _____ a
                             _____ for prayer.

Matthew 14:30   Believers need to _____their prayers
                             to the proper _____ of prayer.

Matthew 6:9–13   Believers need a _____of God's
                             _____ for prayer.

3.   In response to His disciples asking how to pray, Christ revealed six aspects of prayer
      that should be present when following the pattern prayer given by Jesus Christ
      (Matthew 6:9–13).

      Matthew 6:9Be _____with the Father.

      Matthew 6:10Have a _____/_____ for prayer.

      Matthew 6;11Pray that God will _____ your needs.

      Matthew 6:12Practice a _____of prayer.

      Matthew 6:13Seek God's _____through prayer.

      Matthew 6:13Recognize the _____-_____of God.

4.   Make your prayers personal. Concerning the following aspects of prayer, what do you
      include in your personal time(s) of prayer?

      Adoration: Do I worship God when I pray? (1 Chronicles 29:11–13)

                  _____Yes _____ No _____ Not Sure

      Confession: Have I agreed with God concerning my sins and confessed them to God?
      (1 John 1:9)

                  _____Yes _____ No _____ Not Sure

      Forgiveness: Have I given people who have offended me to God? (Mark 11:25;
      Ephesians 4:32)

                  _____Yes _____ No _____ Not Sure

Intercession: Have I offered specific requests to God for others? (Exodus 32:30–32; Daniel 9:18)

_____Yes _____ No _____ Not Sure

Meditation: Have I included God's Word in my prayers? (Psalm 19:7–11)

_____Yes _____ No _____ Not Sure

Surrender: When I pray, am I fully yielded to God? (Romans 12:1; 1 Corinthians 6:20)

_____Yes _____ No _____ Not Sure

Thanksgiving: Have I considered my blessings *and* my trials and given thanks to God for them all to the God who never makes mistakes? (1 Thessalonians 5:18)

_____Yes _____ No _____ Not Sure

5.   Analyze your prayer life. Answer the following questions:

How much time have you spent in prayer

_____ since this morning?
_____ in the last forty-eight hours?

Typically, who is the object of your prayers? (Mark an X.)

_____ yourself
_____ a friend or friends
_____ an acquaintance but not a close friend
_____ a family member
_____ an unsaved person or family
_____ a member or members of the church
_____ all church members (by name)
_____ church attenders who are not members
_____ infrequent church attenders
_____ a Sunday school teacher
_____ a Sunday school child
_____ a Sunday school class
_____ a youth group leader/small group leader
_____ church officers
_____ church boards
_____ a board member

_____ a church committee or committees

_____ the pastor, his wife, and his family

_____ a missionary and his family

_____ national leaders

_____ local leaders

_____ the world situation

_____ other

Typically, what is the purpose of your prayers?

_____ confession of sin

_____ a concern for someone outside the body of Christ

_____ a concern for someone in the family of God

_____ encouragement for church leaders (pastors, etc.)

_____ a personal need

_____ a desire to know Jesus Christ more completely

_____ growing toward spiritual maturity

_____ a family matter

_____ thankfulness

_____ a spiritual need

_____ adoration of God

_____ other requests

6.   From the following Bible passages, what postures can believers take in prayer?

Genesis 18:22 Abraham _____ before the Lord.

Genesis 24:26 God's servant _____ his head.

1 Kings 8:22 Solomon _____ his hands.

1 Chronicles 17:16 David _____ before the Lord.

Matthew 26:39 Jesus Christ _____ on His face.

John 17:1 Jesus Christ _____ _____ His eyes.

Ephesians 3:14 Paul _____ on his knees.

7.   In seventy-five words or fewer, how can you improve your prayer life as to why you pray, when you pray, where you pray, and why you pray?

8.　　　Write out a prayer that includes all the elements of Jesus Christ's pattern prayer.

9.　　　Respond to the following statements on prayer:

The measure of any Christian is his prayer life. (Vance Havner)

The posture of the body is not nearly as important as the posture of the soul. (Source unknown)

There has never been a spiritual awakening in any country or locality that did not begin in united prayer. (Dr. A. T. Pierson)

More things are wrought by prayer than this world dreams of. (Alfred, Lord Tennyson)

Nothing is ever settled until it is settled right, and nothing is ever settled right until it is settled with God in prayer. (Source unknown)

If I should neglect prayer for a single day, I should lose a great deal of the fire of faith. (Martin Luther)

The church must recapture her distinctive. She is not built upon manipulation and money. She is built upon the might of God. If the church is to be light in this perverse generation, she must humble herself and pray. She must understand that victory comes on her knees. (Sammy Tippit)

If all the sleeping folk will wake up … If all the lukewarm folk will fire up … If all the dishonest folk will 'fess up … If all the disgruntled folk will look up … If all the depressed folk will cheer up … If all the estranged folk will make up … If all the gossipers will shut up … If all the true soldiers will stand up … If all the dry bones will shake up … If all the church members will pray up … Then we can have revival. (R. G. Lee)

In relation to His people, God works only in answer to their prayers. (Andrew Murray)

Cares are manifold; therefore let your prayers be manifold. (Charles Haddon Spurgeon)

Groanings that cannot be uttered are often prayers that cannot be refused. (Charles Haddon Spurgeon on Romans 8:26)

Two believers praying the same prayer on earth raises a commotion in heaven. (Source unknown)

You cannot stumble when you are on your knees in prayer. (Source unknown)

He stands best who kneels most. (Source unknown)

The soldiers of the cross do their best fighting on their knees. (Source unknown)

Prayer does not condition God, prayer conditions us. Prayer does not win God to our view, it reveals God's view to us. (Leo Ravenhill)

Even a short prayer will reach the throne, if you don't live too far away. (Source unknown)

There is all the difference in the world between knowing the Word of God and knowing the God of the Word. We know the God of the Word through prayer. (Leo Ravenhill)

What the church needs today is not more machinery or better, nor new organizations or more and novel methods, but men whom the Holy [Spirit] can use -men of prayer, men mighty in prayer. The Holy [Spirit] does not flow through methods, but through men. He does not come on machinery, but on men. He does not anoint plans but men—men of prayer. (E. M. Bounds)

Prayer does not need proof, it needs practice. (Source unknown)

Prayer does not fit us for greater works; prayer is the greater work. We think of prayer as a common sense exercise of our higher powers in order to prepare us for God's work. In the teaching of Jesus Christ, prayer is the working of the miracle of redemption in others by the power of God. (J. Oswald Chambers)

Prayer is releasing the energies of God. For prayer is asking God to do what we cannot do. (Charles Trumbell)

Prayer is the first thing, the second thing, and the third thing necessary for a Christian worker. Pray, then, my dear brother, pray, pray and pray. (Edward Payton)

You can do more than pray *after* you have prayed, but you cannot do more than pray *until* you have prayed. (Source unknown)

Prayer does not change God, prayer changes us. (Charles G. Finney)

Either prayer changes things or prayer changes you. Neither is a bad option. (Selected)

A life built without prayer is like a life built without nails. (Source unknown)

A person may reach heaven without learning, books, or knowledge, but no one ever reached heaven without prayer. (Source unknown)

The church has too many organizers and not enough agonizers; many who pay, buy few who pray; many resters but few wrestlers; many who are enterprising, but too few who are interceding. Those who are not praying are merely playing. (Leo Ravenhill in *No Wonder God Wonders*)

10.   Respond to the following scripture passages on prayer:

My house shall be called the house of prayer. (Matthew 21:13)

If My people, which are called by My name, shall humble themselves, and pray, and seek My face, and turn from their wicked ways; then will I hear from heaven, and will forgive their sin, and will heal their land. (2 Chronicles 7:14)

God forbid that I should sin against the Lord in ceasing to pray for you. (1 Samuel 12:23)

Call unto me, and I will answer Thee, and shew thee great and mighty things, which thou knowest not. (Jeremiah 33:3)

Watch and pray. (Matthew 26:41)

Ask, and it shall be given you; seek, and ye shall find; knock, and it shall be opened unto you. For everyone that asketh receiveth, and he that seeketh findeth, and to him that knocketh it shall be opened. (Matthew 7:7–8)

Men ought always to pray, and not to faint. (Luke 18:1)

Let us therefore come boldly unto the throne of grace, that we may obtain mercy and find grace to help in time of need. (Hebrews 4:16)

Let your requests be made known unto God. And the peace of God which passeth all understanding, shall keep your hearts and minds through Christ Jesus. (Philippians 4:6–7)

This is the confidence that we have in Him, that, if we ask anything according to His will, He heareth us. (1 John 5:14)

Pray without ceasing. (1 Thessalonians 5:17)

If any of you lack wisdom, let him ask of God, Who giveth to all men liberally, and upbraideth not; and it shall be given him. But let him ask in faith, nothing wavering. For he that wavereth is like a wave of the sea driven with the wind and tossed. For let not that man think that he shall receive anything of the Lord. A double-minded man is unstable in all his ways. (James 1:5–8)

Ye have not because ye ask not. (James 4:2)

The effectual fervent prayer of a righteous man availeth much. (James 5:16)

The (Praying) Hand Illustration
Pray will all prayer ...
—Ephesians 6:18

In the praying hand illustration, each finger reminds you to pray for someone specifically. The thumb reminds you to pray for those closest to you. The pointer finger reminds you to pray for people who teach you. The middle finger, because it is the tallest, reminds you to pray for government leaders and others in authority. The fourth finger, because it is the weakest, reminds you to pray for the sick and for those in need of the Savior. The little finger reminds you to pray for yourself.

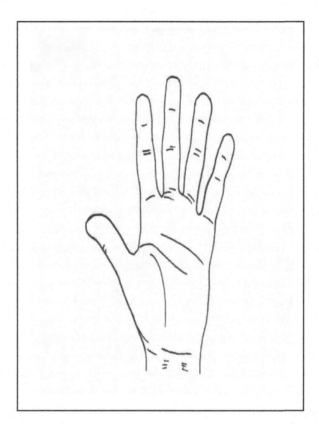

Review. On the above hand illustration, mark the person(s) for whom you are praying. Below, match the digit/finger with the person(s) for whom you are praying.

Thumb   _____

Pointer Finger   _____

Middle Finger   _____

Fourth Finger   _____

Little Finger (Pinkie)   _____

Q: QUIET TIME

Paul wrote,

> All scripture is given by inspiration of God, and is profitable for doctrine (what is right), for reproof (what is not right), for correction (how to get right), and for instruction in righteousness (how to stay right): That the man of God may be perfect (mature and complete), thoroughly furnished unto all good works. (2 Timothy 3:16–17)

> The purpose of this study is to answer five questions concerning a believer's devotional life (quiet time with God).

1.   Why should believers have a daily quiet time with God? Daily Bible study benefits believers for several reasons. (Look up the following passages of scripture, and describe the benefit a study of God's Word provides for the believer.)

Joshua 1:6–8   _____

Psalm 119:9, 11   _____

Psalm 119:105, 130   _____

Proverbs 2:1–5   _____

Jeremiah 15:16   _____

Acts 17:10–14   _____

1 Peter 2:2   _____

2 Timothy 2:15   _____

2.   What should believers include when having a daily quiet time with God? Pick up your Bible. How securely can you grasp it with one finger? How securely can you grasp it with two fingers? You cannot grasp your Bible securely until you get a firm grip with your whole hand. How should believers grab hold of the Word? A hand illustration is an easy-to-remember training tool on getting a firm grasp on the scriptures. (Using the outline of a hand, label each finger with the five words listed in this study).[18]

---

[18]   The "Hand Illustration" is an adaptation of a popular training tool appearing often in the public sector.

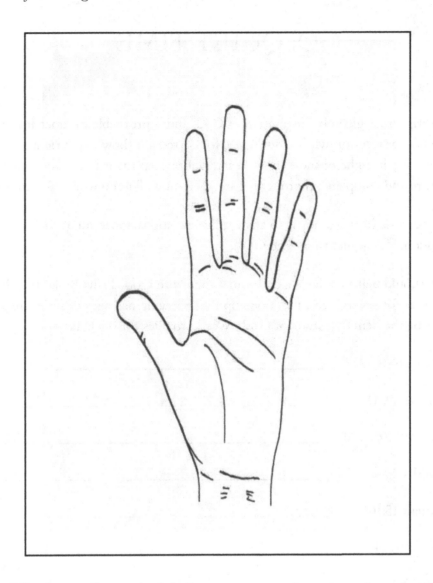

The following are five methods believers can use to learn from the scriptures. (Use the key terms in this section to complete the hand illustration.)

Romans 10:17_____ the Word.

Revelation 1:3_____ the Word.

Acts 17:11_____ the Word.

Psalm 119:9, 11)_____ the Word.

Psalm 1:1–2_____on God's Word.

3.   What questions should a believer ask when meditating on God's Word? Just as
        reporters ask journalistic questions of the events they cover, believers can ask
        questions of God's Word. Select a passage of scripture (Psalm 23 or some other
        passage), and ask the following questions of that passage:

        What was the author's intended meaning?

        What is the immediate and wider context of the passage?

        What type of passage is being studied?

        What is the historical, geographical, and cultural context of the passage?

        What is the grammatical structure of the passage (its hermeneutic)?

        What does the rest of the Bible say about the passage being studies?

4.   In what ways does God's Word benefit the believer? Look up the following passages,
        match each passage to the corresponding truth, and comment on the personal benefit
        you gain from studying God's Word:

        Psalm 19:7–11   _____   A.   It brings new life (conversion) to the soul.

        Psalm 119:9, 11   _____   B.   It builds up the believer in the faith.

        Psalm 119:99   _____   C.   It helps the believer know and understand God's
                                                 truth.

        Psalm 119:105   _____   D.   It helps the believer know right from wrong.

        Matthew 4:4   _____   E.   It keeps the believer from sin.

        John 8:32   _____   F.   It gives direction and guidance to the believer's life.

        John 17:17   _____   G.   It is spiritual bread (food) for the soul (also 1
                                                 Peter 2:2; Hebrews 5:14).

        Acts 17:11   _____   H.   It makes the believer a better worker for God.

        Acts 20:32   _____   I.   It reveals who God (Jesus) is.

        Ephesians 3:19   _____   J.   It gives insight into what is fact and what is false.

        2 Timothy 2:15   _____   K.   It liberates the believer.

Hebrews 5:14 _____ L. It sanctifies believers (sets believers apart from sin).

5.   What study helps are available for use in studying God's Word? Make a list of the study aids mentioned in the author's companion book.

6.   Conduct Bible studies in the following passage types:

- allegorical (Matthew 24–25)—Christ's Olivet discourse/prophecy
- narrative (1 Samuel 17)—David and Goliath
- literal/expository (Ephesians 1:3–14)—Paul's doctrinal teachings

7.   Compare scripture with scripture on the following topics:

- marriage (Genesis 1:21–25; 2:20; Ephesians 5:21–33)
- the home (Deuteronomy 6:4–9; Proverbs 22:6; Ephesians 6:1–4)
- a relationship of grace compared to a religion of works (Galatians)

8.   Conduct some personal Bible studies by applying the information provided in this study.

Study 1: What God Does with Sin

Psalm 32:1

Psalm 32:2

Psalm 103:12

Isaiah 1:18

Isaiah 38:17

Isaiah 43:25

Isaiah 55:7

Micah 7:19

Matthew 26:28

John 1:29

Hebrews 1:3

1 John 1:9

Study 2: Bible Be's

Be _____   Job 22:21

Be _____   Joshua 1:6

Be _____   Matthew 5:48

Be _____   Matthew 14:27

Be _____   Ephesians 4:32

Be _____   James 5:7

Be _____   1 Peter 5:5

Be _____   1 Peter 5:5

Be _____   1 Peter 5:8

Be _____   2 Peter 3:14

Study 3: Some Sure Things

Thou shalt surely _____.   Genesis 2:17

Be sure your _____ will find you out.   Numbers 32:23

The _____ of God standeth sure.   2 Timothy 2:19

The sure word of the _____ of God.   2 Peter 1:19

Surely I _____ quickly.   Revelation 22:20

Notes

R: RELATIONSHIPS

Old Testament Solomon was a man with thousands of relationships. From experience, he wrote,

> Two are better than one; because they have a good reward for their labor. For if they fall, the one will lift up his fellow: but woe to him that is alone when he falleth; for he hath not another to help him up. (Ecclesiastes 4:9–10)

Relationships are important. Scripture describes three common relationships.

1.   The believer's relationships with the unsaved world (government and society) include his connection with people, places, and things. What do the following scripture passages teach concerning the believer's relationship to government and society? Look up the following passages of scripture, and from each passage, describe the believer's responsibilities:

Genesis 1:26–27

Jeremiah 29:7

Acts 5:39

Romans 12:9–21

Romans 13:1–7

Galatians 6:9–10

1 Timothy 2:1–4

Titus 3:1–2

1 Peter 2:13–14

Revelation 21:1–7

2.   In relation to government, answer the following questions:

Is it ever right to oppose the government without a clear biblical directive (Titus 3:2)?

If human authority tells a believer to do something contrary to scripture, should the believer obey God or government (Acts 5:29)?

Do believers have the right to become hostile when unbelievers act like unbelievers (Romans 12:9–21)?

Since the American government model is not a theocracy ("God rule") but a democracy ("people rule"), what else should believers expect from unbelievers?

Is it ever biblical for believers to yield on certain issues that do not count for eternity?

Believers must pick their battles. Should a believer react when the government wants to widen the road or cut down trees? Or should the believer demonstrate restraint and respond to greater moral issues?

How far should a believer go in defending his convictions and in exercising his rights in a society that does not honor God yet desperate needs Him?

If they do not contradict scripture, are there times when believers should submit to government mandates (Shadrach, Meshach, and Abednego—Daniel 3)?

3.   The believer has relationships with his peer groups. Using your Bible, look up the following passages of scripture. Give a description of God's expectations for each relationship. (Answers are in essay form.)

Friendship Relationships (Proverbs 17:17; 18:24; 27:5–6)

Marriage Relationships (Ephesians 5:21–33)

Parent/Child Relationships (Ephesians 6:1–4)

On-the-Job Relationships (Ephesians 6:5–9)

Christian Relationships (Galatians 5:13)

4.　As a community for Jesus Christ, believers are mutually dependent. The relationship between believers is summarized by the "one anothers" of scripture. Most of the "one anothers" are attached to commandments that lead to better relationship in the body of Jesus Christ. From the following passages of scripture, identify the "one another" relationships believers are to have "one with another":

Text	**"One Another"**
Mark 9:50	
John 13:4–5	
John 13:34; 15:12	
Romans 12:5	
Romans 12:10	
Romans 12:16	
Romans 13:8	
Romans 14:13	
Romans 14:19	
Romans 15:5	

Romans 15:7

Romans 15:14

Romans 16:16

1 Corinthians 6:7

1 Corinthians 11:33

1 Corinthians 12:25

Galatians 5:13

Galatians 5:15

Galatians 5:26

Galatians 6:2

Ephesians 4:2

Ephesians 4:25

Ephesians 4:32

Ephesians 5:21

Colossians 3:9

Colossians 3:13

Colossians 3:16

1 Thessalonians 3:12

1 Thessalonians 4:9

1 Thessalonians 4:18

1 Thessalonians 5:11

Titus 3:3

Hebrews 3:13

Hebrews 10:24

James 4:11

James 5:9

James 5:16

1 Peter 1:22

1 Peter 4:9

1 Peter 4:10

1 Peter 5:5

1 John 1:7

1 John 3:11, 23; 4::7, 11, 12

5.   Review the characteristics for each relationship discussed in this study. From 1 (the lowest) to 10 (the highest), rate each of your relationships.

Relationship	Communication	Submission	Understanding of Biblical Function
With friends	_____		
With "spouse"	_____	_____	
With family	_____	_____	
With fellow workers	_____	_____	
With God	_____	_____	

6.   In your marriage relationship, how well do you understand the characteristics and needs of your marriage partner?

Characteristic/Need	Husband	Wife
Basis of success	Success	Relationships

Source of security	Achievement	Relationships
View of home	Place to relax	Place to converse
Affection	Primarily physical	Primarily relational
Priority in "spouse"	Attractive	Integrity (to trust him)
Biblical need	Respect (Ephesians 5:33)	Love (Ephesians5:25–33)
Relationship	Companion	Conversation
Perception	Through analysis	Through feelings

Discussion

7. Respond to these statements: The opposite of love is not hate. It is indifference. When a person hates another person, an emotional attachment remains. Indifference lacks emotional attachment. Whether a person loves you or hates you, a relationship remains. Indifference is what ends the relationship.

8. Respond to this statement: when fulfillment is present, the house becomes a home.

9. The relationship between believers is summarized by the "one anothers" of scripture. Most of the "one anothers" are attached to commandments that lead to better relationships in the body of Jesus Christ. How many of the following "one anothers" from scripture do you practice? Mark an X on the appropriate line in relation to the corresponding "one another."

Mark 9:50   Be at peace one with another.

_____ Yes, I practice this.
_____ No, I do not practice this.
_____ Needs improvement.

John 13:4–5   Wash one another's feet.

_____ Yes, I practice this.
_____ No, I do not practice this.
_____ Needs improvement.

John 13:34; 15:12   Love one another (with agape love).

_____ Yes, I practice this.
_____ No, I do not practice this.

_____ Needs improvement.

Romans 12:5   We are members one of another.

_____ Yes, I practice this.
_____ No, I do not practice this.
_____ Needs improvement.

Romans 12:10   Be kindly affectionate (devoted) to one
                                               another.

_____ Yes, I practice this.
_____ No, I do not practice this.
_____ Needs improvement.

Romans 12:10   Give preference to one another in honor.

_____ Yes, I practice this.
_____ No, I do not practice this.
_____ Needs improvement.

Romans 12:16   Be of the same mind one toward another.

_____ Yes, I practice this.
_____ No, I do not practice this.
_____ Needs improvement.

Romans 13:8   Owe no man anything but to love one
                                               another.

_____ Yes, I practice this.
_____ No, I do not practice this.
_____ Needs improvement.

Romans 14:13   Let us not judge one another.

Yes, I practice this.
No, I do not practice this.
Needs improvement.

Romans 14:19   Edify (build up) one another.

_____ Yes, I practice this.
_____ No, I do not practice this.
_____ Needs improvement.

Romans 15:5   Be like-minded one toward another.

_____ Yes, I practice this.
_____ No, I do not practice this.
_____ Needs improvement.

Romans 15:7   Receive (accept) one another as Christ
                                     received (accepted) us.

_____ Yes, I practice this.
_____ No, I do not practice this.
_____ Needs improvement.

Romans 15:14   Admonish (warn) one another.

_____ Yes, I practice this.
_____ No, I do not practice this.
_____ Needs improvement.

Romans 16:16   Greet (truly welcome) one another.

_____ Yes, I practice this.
_____ No, I do not practice this.
_____ Needs improvement.

1 Corinthians 6:7   Do not go to law one with another.

_____ Yes, I practice this.
_____ No, I do not practice this.
_____ Needs improvement.

1 Corinthians 11:33   Tarry (wait) one for another.

_____ Yes, I practice this.
_____ No, I do not practice this.
_____ Needs improvement.

1 Corinthians 12:25   Have the same care one for another.

_____ Yes, I practice this.
_____ No, I do not practice this.
_____ Needs improvement.

Galatians 5:13   In love, serve one another.

_____ Yes, I practice this.

_____ , I do not practice this.
_____ Needs improvement.

Galatians 5:15   Do not bite and devour (consume) one
                                              another.

_____ Yes, I practice this.
_____ No, I do not practice this.
_____ Needs improvement.

Galatians 5:26   Do not provoke or envy one another.

_____ Yes, I practice this.
_____ No, I do not practice this.
_____ Needs improvement.

Galatians 6:2   Bear one another's burdens.

_____ Yes, I practice this.
_____ No, I do not practice this.
_____ Needs improvement.

Ephesians 4:2   Forebear one another.

_____ Yes, I practice this.
_____ No, I do not practice this.
_____ Needs improvement.

Ephesians 4:25   Speak the truth one to another.

_____ Yes, I practice this.
_____ No, I do not practice this.
_____ Needs improvement.

Ephesians 4:32   Be kind, tenderhearted, and forgiving one
                                              another.

_____ Yes, I practice this.
_____ No, I do not practice this.
_____ Needs improvement.

Ephesians 5:21   Submit (be subject) one to another in the
                                              fear of Christ.

_____ Yes, I practice this.
_____ No, I do not practice this.
_____ Needs improvement.

Colossians 3:9   Lie not one to another.

_____ Yes, I practice this.
_____ No, I do not practice this.
_____ Needs improvement.

Colossians 3:13   Forebear and forgive one another.

_____ Yes, I practice this.
_____ No, I do not practice this.
_____ Needs improvement.

Colossians 3:16   Teach and admonish one another.

_____ Yes, I practice this.
_____ No, I do not practice this.
_____ Needs improvement.

1 Thessalonians 3:12   Abound in love one toward another.

_____ Yes, I practice this.
_____ No, I do not practice this.
_____ Needs improvement.

1 Thessalonians 4:9   Love one another.

_____ Yes, I practice this.
_____ No, I do not practice this.
_____ Needs improvement.

1 Thessalonians 4:18   Comfort (encourage) one another.

_____ Yes, I practice this.
_____ No, I do not practice this.
_____ Needs improvement.

1 Thessalonians 5:11   Encourage one another and build up one another.

_____ Yes, I practice this.
_____ No, I do not practice this.
_____ Needs improvement.

Titus 3:3   Do not hate one another.

_____ Yes, I practice this.

_____ No, I do not practice this.
_____ Needs improvement.

Hebrews 3:13   Exhort (encourage) one another daily.

_____ Yes, I practice this.
_____ No, I do not practice this.
_____ Needs improvement.

Hebrews 10:24   Consider and stimulate one another to
                                             faithfulness.

_____ Yes, I practice this.
_____ No, I do not practice this.
_____ Needs improvement.

James 4:11   Do not speak evil one of another.

_____ Yes, I practice this.
_____ No, I do not practice this.
_____ Needs improvement.

James 5:9   Do not hold a grudge against one
                                             another.

_____ Yes, I practice this.
_____ No, I do not practice this.
_____ Needs improvement.

James 5:16   Confess your sins one to another.

_____ Yes, I practice this.
_____ No, I do not practice this.
_____ Needs improvement.

James 5:16   Pray for one another.

_____ Yes, I practice this.
_____ No, I do not practice this.
_____ Needs improvement.

1 Peter 1:22   Fervently love one another from the
                                             heart.

_____ Yes, I practice this.
_____ No, I do not practice this.
_____ Needs improvement.

1 Peter 4:9   Show hospitality one to another without complaint (grudging).

_____ Yes, I practice this.
_____ No, I do not practice this.
_____ Needs improvement.

1 Peter 4:10   Employ your spiritual gifts in serving one another.

_____ Yes, I practice this.
_____ No, I do not practice this.
_____ Needs improvement.

1 Peter 5:5   Be subject to one another.

_____ Yes, I practice this.
_____ No, I do not practice this.
_____ Needs improvement.

1 John 1:7   Have fellowship one with another.

_____ Yes, I practice this.
_____ No, I do not practice this.
_____ Needs improvement.

1 John 3:11, 23; 4:7, 11, 12   Love one another (with agape) love.

_____ Yes, I practice this.
_____ No, I do not practice this.
_____ Needs improvement.

10. In twenty-five words or fewer, describe your relationship with your friends, marriage partner, family, fellow workers, fellowship group, and God. Over the last month, has it improved, weakened, or stagnated? Over the last year, has your relationship grown stronger, or have you become indifferent?

Relationship with friends over the last month

_____Improved	_____ Grown stronger
_____Weakened	_____ Become indifferent
_____ Stagnated	_____ Other (describe)

Relationship with friends over the last year

_____ Improved	_____ Grown stronger

_____ Weakened   _____ Become indifferent
_____ Stagnated   _____ Other (describe)

Relationship with marriage partner over the last month

_____ Improved   _____ Grown stronger
_____ Weakened   _____ Become indifferent
_____ Stagnated   _____ Other (describe)

Relationship with marriage partner over the last year

_____ Improved   _____ Grown stronger
_____ Weakened   _____ Become indifferent
_____ Stagnated   _____ Other (describe)

Relationship with family over the last month

_____ Improved   _____ Grown stronger
_____ Weakened   _____ Become indifferent
_____ Stagnated   _____ Other (describe)

Relationship with family over the last year

_____ Improved   _____ Grown stronger
_____ Weakened   _____ Become indifferent
_____ Stagnated   _____ Other (describe)

Relationship with fellow workers over the last month

_____ Improved   _____ Grown stronger
_____ Weakened   _____ Become indifferent
_____ Stagnated   _____ Other (describe)

Relationship with fellow workers over the last year

_____ Improved   _____ Grown stronger
_____ Weakened   _____ Become indifferent
_____ Stagnated   _____ Other (describe)

Relationship with fellowship group over the last month

_____ Improved   _____ Grown stronger
_____ Weakened   _____ Become indifferent
_____ Stagnated   _____ Other (describe)

Relationship with fellowship group over the last year

_____ Improved   _____ Grown stronger
_____ Weakened   _____ Become indifferent
_____ Stagnated   _____ Other (describe)

Relationship with God over the last month

_____ Improved   _____ Grown stronger
_____ Weakened   _____ Become indifferent
_____ Stagnated   _____ Other (describe)

Relationship with God over the last year

_____ Improved   _____ Grown stronger
_____ Weakened   _____ Become indifferent
_____ Stagnated   _____ Other (describe)

11.   God made man to have relationships. In the above exercise, in the areas marked "Improved" and "Grown stronger," how can you continue to improve and strengthen these relationships? In the areas marked "Weakened," "Stagnated," "Become indifferent," or "Other," how can you improve these relationships?

S: STEWARDSHIP

Solomon wrote,

> Fear God, and keep His commandments: for this is the whole duty of man. For God shall bring every work into judgment, with every secret thing, whether it be good, or whether it be evil. (Ecclesiastes 12:3–14)

A steward (*oikonomos*) is a *superintendent* or a *manager* of another person's belongings. He is a buyer of goods, an *administrator* of possessions, the *custodian* of another person's household, and a person *entrusted* to manage an owner's estate or to *oversee* a department of that estate.[19] In the Bible, the English term *steward* is mentioned twenty times.

The purpose of this study is to examine the biblical stewardships that God has entrusted to believers. The Bible speaks of five specific stewardships.

1.   The stewardship of the gospel: Have you been a faithful steward of the gospel? When was the last time you made an intentional effort to speak to someone about Jesus Christ? Jesus Christ's stated purpose for every believer is to "make disciples" (Matthew 28:19). Believers are born to reproduce. Have you been faithful?

   Make this commitment. Since stewards are required to be faithful, I will be faithful in sharing the gospel of Jesus Christ.

   Signature _____

2.   The stewardship of your spiritual gifts: Which gifts do you possess? Of these gifts, which gifts are you investing in service in the body of Jesus Christ? Are you fully yielded to the Holy Spirit's control in the area of using your gifts and talents for the Lord?

   Make this commitment. Since stewards are required to be faithful, I will be faithful in using my spiritual gifts to further the kingdom and cause of Jesus Christ.

   Signature _____

3.   The stewardship of God's Word: Do your faithfully read God's Word? Do you study God's Word? Do you faithfully obey and apply God's Word to your life by living out its truths?

---

[19]   Colin Brown, ed. *Dictionary of New Testament Theology*, "House," by J. Goetzmann, s.v., *"oikonomos,"* 2:253–256.

Make this commitment. Since stewards are required to be faithful, I will be faithful in reading God's Word and applying His Word to my life.

Signature _____

4.   The stewardship of your generation: How do you invest your time? How much time do you spend with God, your marriage partner, and your children? How much time do you spend on the job, in rest and relaxation, on hobbies, and in recreation? How much time do you invest in ministry, with friends? How much of your time is wasted? How much of your time is managed around the Lord? Do you give a tithe of your time to God? Of the time you invest with God, on yourself, or with others, how much of that time is "quality" time?

Make this commitment. Since stewards are required to be faithful, I will be faithful in using my time as an investment for the kingdom and cause of Jesus Christ.

Signature _____

5.   The stewardship of giving: Believers are bought with a price (1 Corinthians 6:19–20). God wants each believer to acknowledge God's ownership on his life. Make this commitment. Since stewards are required to be faithful, I will be faithful in giving of my substance to God.

Signature _____

6.   On the topic of giving, from the following scripture passages, give two guidelines for faithful giving:

1 Corinthians 16:1 Giving must be _____.

1 Corinthians 16:2 Giving is a_____ for every believer.

7.   On the topic of giving, answer the following questions:

When should believers give?

How can a believer calculate his giving?

Who should give to God?

How should believers give?

8.   What are some additional truths revealed in the Bible concerning the stewardship of finances? The Bible reveals truths about giving. Look up each passage, and from each passage, explain the truth(s) about giving.

Deuteronomy 8:18	All finances come from _____ (that man's God is concerned about your money).
Proverbs 13:11	Spend _____ than you earn and do it for a long time and you will be successful financially (Proverbs 13:11).
Proverbs 21:20	The way believers spend their money must be _____ to God.
Proverbs 28:19–20	Money must be obtained by _____ means. (Honest means are means that please and honor God.)
Psalm 37:21	Whenever you borrow money for any reason, there must be a _____ way to pay it back (Psalm 37:21).
Luke 16:11–12	Money is first a tool, then a test, then a _____.
John 3:16	When God gives, He gives His _____.
2 Corinthians 8:1–9	Believers should be _____ givers.
Philippians 4:19	God will _____ for His own.
1 Timothy 6:7–20	People who give (lovers of grace), _____ God more than their money.

9.   Examine the following statements, and mark an X on the appropriate lines:

The stewardship of the gospel: I am a faithful witness for Jesus (verbally and in living).

_____ Yes _____ No _____ Needs Improvement

The stewardship of my spiritual gifts: I am faithful in using my spiritual gifts for Jesus Christ.

_____ Yes _____ No _____ Needs Improvement

The stewardship of God's Word: I am faithful in reading and applying God's Word.

_____ Yes _____ No _____ Needs Improvement

The stewardship of this generation: I am faithful in investing my time for the Lord.

_____ Yes _____ No _____ Needs Improvement

The stewardship of giving: I am faithful in giving back to God what I owe to Him.

_____ Yes _____ No _____ Needs Improvement

10.   Rank your priorities (1 is the highest, 10 is the lowest, and ties are allowed):

_____ God
_____ family
_____ friends
_____ marriage
_____ job
_____ money
_____ recreation
_____ entertainment
_____ church
_____ serving Jesus (using my spiritual gifts)
_____ better use of time
_____ witnessing
_____ prayer
_____ rest and relaxation (leisure time)
_____ time with God
_____ giving
_____ time with friends

11.   Do you give of your finances to God? _____ Yes _____ No
Do you tithe?   _____ Yes _____ No
Do you tithe and give an offering?   _____ Yes _____ No

12.   12.God loves cheerful givers (2 Corinthians 9:6–8). I commit myself to giving a tithe and an offering of what I earn to the Lord.

Signature _____

Notes

13.   For yourself or for your family, make a budget that reflects the values of scripture.

Annual income: $
Annual expenses:

        To God (10 percent plus an offering): $
        To Government (taxes, etc.) $

Total working funds remaining: $

        10 percent to savings $
        20 percent to debts/loans $
        70 percent to living expenses $

Worksheet (for living expenses): $

        Debts and loans: $
        Lodging: $
        Transportation: $
        Other: $

Food:

        Groceries (market) $
        Other: $

Home:

        Utilities: $
        Other: $

Transportation:

        Fuel: $
        Upkeep: $
        Other: $

Insurance:

        Auto: $
        Health: $
        Life: $
        Other: $
Medical: $
Clothing: $
Education: $

    Recreation/vacation: $

    Miscellaneous: $

Total living expenses (to place on line above):$_

Necessary adjustments to income/budget:$

14.   In thirty words or fewer, describe yourself as a steward.

WEEKLY SCHEDULE (CHART)
Redeeming the time for the days are evil.
—Ephesians 5:16

Special note: Chart your week. From your schedule, identify your priorities. Are your priorities consistent with the priorities presented in scripture? Are all five stewardship priorities reflected in your schedule? What should you add? What should eliminate (do without)?

Time	Sunday	Monday	Tuesday	Wednesday	Thursday	Friday	Saturday
6 a.m.							
7 a.m.							
8 a.m.							
9 a.m.							
10 a.m.							
11 a.m.							
Noon							
1 p.m.							
2 p.m.							
3 p.m.							
4 p.m.							
5 p.m.							
6 p.m.							
7 p.m.							
8 p.m.							
9 p.m.							
10 p.m.							
11 p.m.							
Midnight– 6 a.m.							

T: TRIALS

James wrote,

> My brethren, count it all joy when ye fall into [various testings]; knowing this, that the trying of your faith [produces] patience. [Therefore] let [patient endurance] have her perfect work, that ye may be [mature] and [complete in character], [lacking in nothing that counts for God]. (James 1:2–4)

The purpose of this study is to ask and answer three questions about the trials of a believer's faith.

1.   What are trials? The Bible uses several words for trials and then uses picture words to bring those trials to life. Look up the passages of scripture, and identify the terms for trials.

John 16:33_____

2 Timothy 3:12_____

Hebrews 11:25 _____

1 Peter 1:7_____

2.   The Bible pictures trials in seven ways. Look up the passage of scripture, and identify the ways God pictures trials. In which of these ways are you being tried?

Job 19:11–12 The testing experience is pictured as a _____.

Job 23:10 The testing experience is pictured as a _____.

Psalm 69:1–2 The testing experience is pictured as a _____.

Isaiah 48:10 The testing experience is pictured as a _____.

Jeremiah 4:31 The testing experience is pictured as a _____.

Jeremiah 12:7 The testing experience is pictured as _____ _____.

Matthew 23:12 The testing experience is pictured as a _____.

3.   What reasons does the Bible give for the believer's afflictions? Take your Bible. Look up the references. Describe why believers suffer.

Job 2:10   Believers suffer because suffering is a

_____ __ _____.

Psalm 119:67, 71   Believers suffer because suffering helps the believer
_____ God's Word.

Isaiah 43:2–5   Believers suffer to create a greater _____ of the
presence of Christ.

Acts 14:22   Believers suffer because suffering is _____ for
with 2 Timothy 3:12   believers.

Romans 5:3–5   Believers suffer because trials _____ character.

Romans 8:18   Believers suffer because of the promise of
future _____.

Romans 8:22–23   Believers suffer because of original _____.

Romans 8:28   Believers suffer because God wants believers to see the
_____ _____ in life.

Romans 12:1–2   Believers suffer because God wants to _____
believers to the image and character of His Son.

2 Corinthians 1:4   Believers suffer because believers who suffer can _____
other people who suffer.

Hebrews 12:6–8, 11   Believers suffer because trials are a vital part of God's hand
of _____ in the life of the believer (trials help the
believer _____ in the faith).

James 1:2–4   Believers suffer so believers can _____.

1 Peter 4:19   Believers suffer because trials increase the
_____ to serve and please Jesus Christ.

1 Peter 5:8   Believers suffer because the _____wants believers to
deny Jesus Christ.

4.   Look up the following passages of scripture, and compile a list of people in scripture who experienced trials. For each, answer the following questions: What was the trial? How did the individual(s) respond? What lessons did the individual(s) learn? What can you learn from the person's trial? (A starter list is provided.)

Text	Person(s) Involved in the Trial	Circumstance/Lesson(s)
Genesis 37–50		
Job		
The Psalms		
Daniel 1, 6		
Daniel 3		
Acts 7		
Acts 13–28		
Revelation 7		

5.   What/who causes you stress?

6.   How can you overcome stress (Psalm 37:1–8)?

Psalm 37:1   Do not _____.
Psalm 37:3   _____ in the Lord (have faith).
Psalm 37:4   _____ in the Lord.
Psalm 37:5   _____ your plans to the Lord.
Psalm 37:7   _____ your circumstance to God.
Psalm 37:23   _____ God to order your steps.

7.   Describe a recent time of testing. What was the test? What passages did God use to help you through your trial? What did you learn because of your time of testing?

U: UNITY

David wrote,

> Behold, how good and how pleasant it is for brethren to dwell together in unity. It is like the precious ointment upon the head, that ran down upon the beard, even Aaron's beard: that went down to the skirts of his garments; as the dew of Hermon and as the dew that descended upon the mountains of Zion: for there the Lord commanded the blessing, even life forevermore. (Psalm 133:1–3)

The purpose of this study is to enhance the believer's appreciation of the unity and fellowship he enjoys in his "body life" for Jesus Christ. God loves a healthy church.

1. God wants believers to promote unity in the body of Jesus Christ, His church. In the following passage on unity (Ephesians 4:4–6), what phrases does Paul use to describe the church's unity. What does each phrase mean?

    One B_____: The parts of Christ's Body are to work together as one.

    One S_____: God's Holy Spirit is the power that promotes unity in the church.

    One H_____: Hope is the promise of the believer's future home with Christ.

    One L_____: Jesus Christ is the Person believers worship and serve.

    One F_____: Faith is the believer's personal dependence on Jesus Christ.

    One B_____: Holy Spirit baptism places believers into the body of Christ.

    One G_____ and F_____: A unified body recognizes the preeminence of God the Father.

2.   There are twenty-three New Testament phrases that describe the unity God wants in His church. What are those phrases? Are you practicing this part of God's plan for your life? Look up each reference in your Bible. Then place an X on the appropriate line under each text.

Unified believers are comforted together (Romans 1:12).
Are you? _____ Yes _____ No _____ Needs improvement

Unified believers are planted together (Romans 6:5).
Are you? _____ Yes _____ No _____ Needs improvement

Unified believers are glorified together (Romans 8:17).
Are you? _____ Yes _____ No _____ Needs improvement

Unified believers are striving together (Romans 15:30).
Are you? _____ Yes _____ No _____ Needs improvement

Unified believers are joined together (1 Corinthians 1:10).
Are you? _____ Yes _____ No _____ Needs improvement

Unified believers are laborers together (1 Corinthians 3:9).
Are you? _____ Yes _____ No _____ Needs improvement

Unified believers are gathered together (1 Corinthians 5:4).
Are you? _____ Yes _____ No _____ Needs improvement

Unified believers are coming together (1 Corinthians 11:33).
Are you? _____ Yes _____ No _____ Needs improvement

Unified believers are helping together (2 Corinthians 1:11).
Are you? _____ Yes _____ No _____ Needs improvement

Unified believers are workers together (2 Corinthians 6:1).
Are you? _____ Yes _____ No _____ Needs improvement

Unified believers are yoked together (2 Corinthians 6:14).
Are you? _____ Yes _____ No _____ Needs improvement

Unified believers are quickened/brought to life together (Ephesians 2:5).
Are you? _____ Yes _____ No _____ Needs improvement

Unified believers are raised up together (Ephesians 2:6).
Are you? _____ Yes _____ No _____ Needs improvement

Unified believers are framed together (Ephesians 2:21).
Are you? _____ Yes _____ No _____ Needs improvement

Unified believers are "builded" together (Ephesians 2:22).
Are you? _____ Yes _____ No _____ Needs improvement

Unified believers are contending together (Philippians 1:27).
Are you? _____ Yes _____ No _____ Needs improvement

Unified believers are followers together (Philippians 3:17).
Are you? _____ Yes _____ No _____ Needs improvement

Unified believers are knit together (Colossians 2:2).
Are you? _____ Yes _____ No _____ Needs improvement

Unified believers are caught up together (1 Thessalonians 4:17).
Are you? _____ Yes _____ No _____ Needs improvement

Unified believers are living peaceably together (1 Thessalonians 5:10).
Are you? _____ Yes _____ No _____ Needs improvement

Unified believers are assembling together (Hebrews 10:25).
Are you? _____ Yes _____ No _____ Needs improvement

Unified believers are heirs together (1 Peter 3:7).
Are you? _____ Yes _____ No _____ Needs improvement

Unified believers are elected together (1 Peter 5:13).
Are you? _____ Yes _____ No _____ Needs improvement

3.   God wants believers to have fellowship in the body of Jesus Christ. There are five New Testament terms for *fellowship*. All five all appear in 2 Corinthians 6:4–16. List and define the five terms.

F_____ (*metokee*, seven New Testament appearances)

C_____ (*koinania*, twenty-nine New Testament appearances)

C_____ (*sumphoneesis*, eight New Testament appearances)

P_____ (*meris*, ten New Testament appearances)

A_____ (*sunkatathesis*, two New Testament appearances)

4.   From the following passages, what destroys unity? What divides a fellowship?

      John 17:15   _____

      Romans 12:16–21   _____

      Romans 14:3   _____

      Galatians 5:17–20   _____

      Ephesians 4:14   _____

      Colossians 3:5–11   _____

      James 2:1–11   _____

5.   What do the following passages teach about unity and fellowship?

      2 Chronicles 30:12   _____

      Psalm 133:1–2   _____

      John 17:20–23   _____

      Acts 2:46   _____

      Romans 12:4   _____

      Romans 15:5–6   _____

      1 Corinthians 11:23–34   _____

      2 Corinthians 6:14–7:1   _____

      Galatians 3:26–29   _____

      Ephesians 4:1–6   _____

      Ephesians 4:11–16   _____

      Philippians 2:5–8   _____

      Colossians 2:2–3   _____

      1 Peter 3:8–11   _____

      Revelation 19:9   _____

6.   What do the following passages teach concerning the believer's biblical response to people who continue to compromise the testimony of God's true church?

Matthew 18:15–18

_____

_____

_____

Romans 16:17

_____

_____

_____

1 Corinthians 5:9–10

_____

_____

_____

1 Thessalonians 5:14

_____

_____

_____

2 Thessalonians 3:5–6

_____

_____

_____

Titus 3:9–11

_____

_____

_____

7.   In fifty words or fewer, describe how can you demonstrate a spirit of unity and fellowship among God's people?

8.   From the following list, establish your top seven personal core values. Then, backed by scripture, establish the church's top seven corporate core values. Of your top seven personal core values, how many match the church's top seven corporate core values? (The core values that match are called "shared" core values). Churches with members who submit their personal core values to the core values of the church as a whole, in all probability, are attending a church that practices biblical unity).Underline your top seven personal core values. Circle the church's top seven corporate core values. Determine which values are shared core values. Then, to establish or maintain unity, submit your personal core values to the church's core values.

Leadership	Evangelism	Discipleship
Family	Friends	Fellowship
Prayer	Bible Teaching/Preaching	
Community	Fun	Personal choice
Rights	Worship	Stewardship
Building and Grounds	Justice	Missions
Cultural Relevance	Maintaining	Appreciation
Ministries of service	Mutual support	Counseling
Benevolence (social concerns	Comfort	Commitment
Conformity	Achievement	Belonging
Cleanliness	Balance	Reconciliation
Education	Excellence	Creativity
Generosity	Health	Work/The Job
Grace	Love	Obedience
Passion	Faith	Hope
Integrity	Sound doctrine	Growth
Growth	Loyalty	Peace
Patience/Long-suffering	Temperance	Open-mindedness
Peace	Recreation	Devotion
Depth	Efficiency	Support
Energy	Enthusiasm	Holiness
Happiness	Joy	Pleasure
Maturity	Organization	Purity
Sacrifice	Sensitivity	Stability
Truth	Wisdom	Traditions
Respect	Worship	Reverence
Music	Forgiveness	Unity
Healthy	Relationships Mercy	My pride
Gentleness (common courtesy)	Goodness	Goodness
Faithfulness to God	Self-control	Integrity
A virtuous life	Work/The Job	My Social Life
My Personal Space	Bible Knowledge	Kindness
Compassion Ministries	What I want to do with my life	
God's Will	Biblical Authority	(Other)

Additional study: From the above selections, list your top seven personal values, God's top seven core values for you, the personal core values that are shared core values with God, what you think the church's top seven core values should be, and—for the sake of church unity—your personal core values that you must submit to the church's core values (when you enter the building).

Personal Values	God's Core Values (7)Values for You	Shared Core (7)Values	Church's Core Values	Core Values You Should Submit
1.	1.	1.	1.	1.
2.	2.	2.	2.	2.
3.	3.	3.	3.	3.
4.	4.	4.	4.	4.
5.	5.	5.	5.	5.
6.	6.	6.	6.	6.
7.	7.	7.	7.	7.

V: VICTORY

John wrote, "For whatsoever is born of God overcometh the world: and this is the victory that overcometh the world, even our faith[fulness to Jesus Christ]" (1 John 5:4). The purpose of this study is to examine the source of believers' sins (identify sin as sin) and to discover the secret(s) to resisting temptation.

1.   What is sin? From the following scripture references, identify the names for sin:

Text	Name for Sin	Meaning of the Name
Matthew 6:12D	_____ [*ophilee*]	A debt or something that is owed
Matthew 6:15T	_____ [*paraptoma*]	An unintentional slip; an offense against God's character or nature
Matthew 7:23	I_____ [*anomia*]	To willfully break God's established rules
Matthew 18:17	Refuse to h_____	An intentional "closing of the ears" to God [*parakouo*] (saying no to God)
Acts 17:30	I_____ [*agnoia*]	Not knowing what you should have known
Romans 3:23; 5:8	S____ [*hamartia*]	Missing the mark of God's holy expectations
Romans 5:19;	D_____ [*parakoee*]	A refusal to obey God and His Word
1 Corinthians 6:7	F_____[*heeteema*]	To de-emphasize or diminish what God considers important
Titus 2:12	U_____ [*asebia*]	Anything that violates the holiness of God
James 2:9, 11	T_____ [*parabasis*]	To intentionally cross the line established by God and go beyond God's established limits of behavior

1 Peter 2:25   Gone _____ [*planao*]   A wandering by forsaking the right path

1 John 1:9; 5:17   U_____ [*adikia*]   Wrongdoings

2.   What is temptation? What does the Bible say concerning temptation? From the following scripture passages, determine God's truth(s) concerning temptation:

Text	Truth(s)
Psalm 119:9–11	
Matthew 6:13	
Luke 22:31–32	
1 Corinthians 10:13	
Ephesians 4:27	
Ephesians 6:11	
James 4:7–8	
1 Peter 5:8–10	
1 John 2:1–2	
1 John 4:4	
1 John 5:3–5	

3.   Who was tempted, in scripture? From the following scripture passages, identify the person(s) who were tempted to sin. Did the person pass or fail his "temptation test"?

Text	Person(s) Tempted	Temptation	Pass/Fail
Genesis 3:1–6			
Genesis 12:10–20			
Genesis 13:5–11			
Genesis 22			
Genesis 26:6–16			

Genesis 27:1–33

Genesis 39:1–23

Exodus 32:1–10

Numbers 20:11

Joshua 7:1–27

Judges 16:4–22

1 Samuel 24, 26

2 Samuel 11

2 Chronicles 32

Job 2:10

Daniel 1

Daniel 3

Matthew 4:4

4.   Believers are God's conquering sheep (Romans 8:37). In what ways can believers overcome temptation and gain victory over sin? Look up the following scripture references, and identify ways to overcome temptation:

Text	Way to Overcome Temptation
Psalm 1:1–3;	
Proverbs 13:20;	
1 Corinthians 15:33	
Psalm 119:9, 11	
Matthew 6:9–13	
Romans 13:14	
2 Corinthians 5:9–11	

2 Corinthians 6:14–7:1

2 Timothy 2:22

James 1:12

James 5:16

5.   Scripture's classic passage on combating the influences of temptation is Ephesians 6:10–17. From this passage, how can believers gain victory over temptation? Examine the scripture passages and identify the ways believers can gain victory over temptation and sin.

      Ephesians 6:10–12   Be adequately _____.

      Ephesians 6:13–17   Be properly _____.

6.   What should believers wear to the spiritual battle? From the following scripture passages, identify the believer's armor:

      Ephesians 6:14   Wear the_____ of _____.

      Ephesians 6:14   Wear the _____ (chest piece) of _____.

      Ephesians 6:15   Wear the protective _____ of _____.

      Ephesians 6:16   Carry the _____ of _____.

      Ephesians 6:17   Put on the _____ of _____.

      Ephesians 6:17   Use the _____of the _____.

7.   From the following passage, identify another powerful way to overcome temptation:

      Ephesians 6:18   Be _____through _____.

8.   Look up the following passages. What blessings were given to believers who overcame temptation, compromise, and sin?

      Text   **Blessing(s)**

      Revelation 2:7

      Revelation 2:11

      Revelation 2:17

      Revelation 2:26–27

      Revelation 3:6

      Revelation 3:12

      Revelation 3:21

9.   Describe a recent temptation. How did you handle it? Did you gain victory? If so, what scripture passages did God use to help you overcome your temptation?

W: WORSHIP

David had a heart that was filled with God. He wrote, "O come, let us worship and bow down, let us kneel before the Lord our Maker" (Psalm 95:6). The purpose of this study is to define worship, to discover some principles for worship, and to determine how believers can worship God.

1.   What is worship? From the following scripture passages, define biblical worship:

Worship is _____ the _____ of God. (Luke 10:38–42).

Worship is the believer's highest _____ John 4:23).

Worship is _____ (Revelation 5:11, 12, 14).

Worship is the believer's ___-_____ with God (Matthew 6:9).

2.   What are the principles of genuine, authentic worship? There are seven words in the Bible that describe a believer's worship. From the following scripture passages, describe biblical worship:

Genesis 22:5   Worship is described as _____ down [*shachah*].

Daniel 3:5   Worship is described as _____ down [*sagheed*].

Matthew 2:2   Worship is described as _____-_____ (kissing a person's hand: [*proskuneo*]).

Matthew 2:11   Worship is described as _____ [*sebomai*].

Acts 17:25   Worship is described as menial _____ [*therapeuo*].

Ephesians 1:6   Worship is described as _____ _____ [*doxa*].

Philippians 3:3   Worship is described as _____ [*latreuo*].

3.   What are some characteristics of true and authentic worship? From the following scripture passages, describe what God "looks for" when believers worship Him:

Exodus 3:5 with Joshua 5:15   True worship recognizes its place is

_____ _____.

Exodus 33:13–15   True worship _____ the _____ of God.

Isaiah 6:1–8　　　　　　True worship is from a _____ heart.

Hebrews 13:15　　　　　True worship includes_____ from the heart.

Revelation 4–5　　　　　True worship is _____ toward Jesus.

4.　How should believers worship God? Who, in the Bible, worshipped God? From the following scripture passages, determine who worshiped God and how he worshiped:

Text	Person Who Worshiped	How the Person(s) Worshiped
Genesis 12:8		
Genesis 18:23–33		
Genesis 28:20–22		
Psalm 96:9		
Isaiah 6:3		
Daniel 6:10		
Matthew 2:1–8		
John 12:1–8		

5.　How do you worship God?

6.　Worship styles have changed with each generation. In years past, formal worship was honored. In modern days, casual worship is the norm. Study the following chart of "Then" and "Now" worship. What is the emphasis of your church's corporate worship? What is the emphasis of your personal worship to God?

Category	Worship Then	Worship Now
musictraditional	hymnscontemporary	praise
instrument(s)	piano and organ	band
medium	song books	media (slides)
director	song leader	worship leader
volume	softer	louder
preaching	sermon	message
announcements	bulletin	worship folder

lighting	adequate	dark
approach	informative	celebrative
singers	choir	praise team
planning	structured	flexible
goal	worship	worship
other:		

Your church's worship (place an X next to the appropriate words):

Your personal worship (circle the appropriate words):

7. From the following list, what is your preferred worship style? Is your preferred worship style consistent with what God wants in worship?

Liturgical worship (structured with forms). See the following Old Testament examples: Leviticus 23; Joel 1:2–3, 14; 2:12–16; and other days of consecration to the Lord. This worship form has been typical of the following church movements: Roman Catholic, Episcopalian, Church of England, Anglican, and Lutheran.

Traditional worship (structured with fewer forms). Typically traditional worship includes meditation (Psalm 63:3–4), music (Ephesians 5:19), prayer (1 Timothy 2:1–8. giving (1 Corinthians 16:1–2), praise (Hebrews 13:15), a Bible message (2 Timothy 4:1–2), and a time for dedication (2 Corinthians 6:14–7:1). This model has more flexibility than fixed liturgies and historically has been practiced by the following church groups: Baptist, Methodist, and the Bible church movement.

Celebrative worship (praise worship). This model happens in a nonthreatening worship environment and places emphasis on felt needs, drama, songs of adoration, a believer's ministry to God, and informal, nontraditional styles. Bible instruction is included at various times during the worship experience. The forerunners of this worship movement were the following church groups: Charismatic, Pentecostal, and Vineyard.

Syncretistic worship (a combination of a variety of popular worship forms). This model places emphasis on connecting with people and does not necessarily base its forms on scripture but rather on what draws people from a secular society. "Post-Christian" churches often practice this form of convergence worship.

8. From the following passages, list some obstacles to worship:

Matthew 5:22–23   An _____ _____

Acts 17:23   _____

1 John 1:9   _____ _____

1 John 2:15–17   The _____

1 Peter 5:8   _____

9.   On your own: In what ways has your worship experience resulted in blessings for your life? What do you derive from your worship experience? How can you improve your personal and corporate worship experiences?

10.   New Testament Mary and Old Testament Hannah each had a son who honored God and had their words of worship recorded as scripture. For your personal enjoyment, compare Mary's Magnificat in Luke 1:46–55 with Hannah's Hymn in 1 Samuel 2:1–10.

Mary's Magnificat (Luke 1:46–55)	**Hannah's Hymn (1 Samuel 2:1–10)**
(46) My soul doth magnify the Lord	(1) My heart rejoiceth in the Lord
(47) And my spirit hath rejoiced in God my Savior	(1) Mine horn is exalted in the Lord
(51) He hath showed strength with His arm	(4) The bows of the mighty men are broken
(52) He hath scattered the proud in the imagination of their hearts girded with strength	(4) They that stumbled are
(52) He hath put down the mighty from their seats	(6) The Lord killeth and maketh alive
(52) He exalted them of low degree	(6) He bringeth down to the grave and bringeth up
(53) He hath filled the hungry with good things	(5) They that were full hath hired themselves out for bread
(53) The rich He hath sent away empty	(5) They that were hungry ceased

X: X-RAY

Paul wrote, "Examine yourselves, whether ye be in the faith; [and] prove your own selves" (2 Corinthians 13:5). The purpose of this study is to describe two characteristics of the future examination of every believer at the judgment seat of Jesus Christ.

1.   As you begin to examine your relationship with Jesus Christ, ask yourself these questions:

   O Is your profession of faith genuine and authentic (1 John 2:3–9)?
   O Are you making progress in your growth toward spiritual maturity (1 John 2:12–14; 2 Peter 3:18)?
   O Are you practicing Christianity (1 John 2:29)?
   O Is your teaching consistent with scripture (1 John 4:1–4)?

2.   The Bible speaks of five judgments. Each is significant based on a person's salvation response to Jesus. Most are for believers. Several are for unbelievers. From the following chart, identify each judgment, the location of the judgment, who is judged, and what is judged:

Text	Judgment	Location	Who Is Judged	What Is Judged
John 5:24	Sin	Cross	All	The Soul
1 Corinthians 11:31–32	Self	Communion	Believer	Lifestyles
Romans 14:12; 1 Corinthians 3:12–15; 2 Corinthians 5:9	Service	Bema seat	Believers	Motivations
Joel 3:13–16	Society	Armageddon	Nations	Response to Jesus
Revelation 20:11–15	Souls	Great White Throne	The Lost	Rejection of Jesus

3.   What can the believer know about the Bema seat judgment? Ask yourself the following journalistic questions. Scripture provides the answers.

   O When does the believer's examination take place (Matthew 16:27; Revelation 22:12)?
   O Where does the believer's examination take place (1 Thessalonians 4:17; Revelation 4:2; 1 Corinthians 3:12–15)?
   O Who is the Judge at the believer's examination (John 5:22; Romans 2:16; 2 Timothy 4:8)?
   O Who is examined at the Bema seat of Jesus Christ (1 Corinthians 3:12–16; 2 Corinthians 5:10; 1 John 2:28)?

    ○ How are believers examined (John 5:24; 12:31; Romans 8:1; Hebrews 12:6; 2 Corinthians 5:10)?

4.   What will God judge? From the following scripture passages, determine what God will judge:

Psalm 19:17   The believer's _____.

John 5:22–23   The believer's _____.

2 Corinthians 5:10   The believer's _____.

5.   In your own words, what happens at the time of the believer's Bema seat examination (1 Corinthians 3:2–15)?

6.   From the following scripture passages, what rewards does God give believers to cast at the feet of Jesus?

1 Corinthians 9:24–27

1 Thessalonians 2:19

James 1:12; Revelation 2:10

2 Timothy 4:8

1 Peter 5:4

7.   Paul describes a fire in heaven (1 Corinthian 3:12–16). What six elements are placed into the fire? What does each element symbolize?

Element	What the Element Symbolizes
Gold	Matthew 2:11
Silver	Proverbs 10:20
Precious Stones	Exodus 28:17
Wood	Jeremiah 5:13–14
Hay	Isaiah 40:6
Stubble	Job 13:25

8. What is your mind-set? What are your motives? What is your ministry? What are your methods?

9. In your own words, describe the scene at the Bema seat of Jesus Christ. What do you expect? What do you see? Are there sins in your life that need to be confessed? What will you say when Jesus Christ asks you to give a verbal report of your thoughts, words, and actions? Are you properly motivated? (Were you motivated by love for Jesus Christ?) Have you been faithful to Jesus Christ?

10. God said to "judge ourselves" so that we should not be judged (1 Corinthians 11:31). In the spirit of self-examination, judge yourself in the following categories. (Place an X on the appropriate lines.)

The exercise and use of my spiritual gifts (Matthew 25:14–28; 1 Peter 4:10)

_____ Rewards _____ Rebuke _____ Not Sure

Faithful service to Jesus Christ (1 Corinthians 4:1–6; 9:24–27)

_____ Rewards _____ Rebuke _____ Not Sure

My generosity in giving (2 Corinthians 9:6; 1 Timothy 6:17–19)

_____ Rewards _____ Rebuke _____ Not Sure

Christlikeness in my life. "Holding forth the Word of life" (Philippians 2:16)

_____ Rewards _____ Rebuke _____ Not Sure

Leading souls to Jesus Christ (1 Thessalonians 2:19)

_____ Rewards _____ Rebuke _____ Not Sure

Looking forward to the coming of Jesus Christ (2 Timothy 4:8)

_____ Rewards _____ Rebuke _____ Not Sure

Respect for people in authority (Hebrews 13:7, 17; 1 Thessalonians 5:12–13)

_____ Rewards _____ Rebuke _____ Not Sure

Faithfully enduring trials (James 1:12; Revelation 2:10)

_____ Rewards _____ Rebuke _____ Not Sure

11.   10.At His first coming, Jesus Christ was mocked, beaten, and crucified. At His Second Coming, every knee will bow and every tongue confess that Jesus Christ is Lord (Isaiah 45:23; Philippians 2:10–11). Where do you stand with Jesus today?

Y: YIELDING TO GOD

Paul wrote,

> Likewise reckon ye also yourselves to be dead indeed unto sin, but alive unto God through Jesus Christ our Lord. Let not sin therefore reign in your mortal body, that ye should obey it in the lusts thereof. Neither yield ye your members as instruments of unrighteousness unto sin: but yield yourselves unto God, as those that are alive from the dead, and your members as instruments of righteousness unto God. (Romans 6:11–13)

Yielding to God involves satisfying God's will. The purpose of this study is to examine God's will for your life and to measure your yieldedness to it.

1.   God has a general will for every believer. Much of God's general will for your daily existence is revealed in scripture Look up each passage of scripture. Then identify the will of God for your life.

Text	God's Will for Your Life
Proverbs 3:5–8	
Romans 12:1–2	
Ephesians 5:18	
1 Thessalonians 4:3–7	
1 Timothy 2:4	
1 Peter 2:13–15	
Ephesians 5:21	
1 Peter 3:17; 4:19	

2.   In the Old Testament's classic passage on yielding to God's will, Solomon revealed four conditions that must be met for believers to enjoy the leading of the Lord (Proverbs 3:5–8). List those conditions.

Proverbs 3:5   The believer must _____ ___ (trust) God to give His best.

Proverbs 3:5   The believer must _____ his entire weight of his life on God.

Proverbs 3:6   The believer must _____ that God's presence is with him always.

Proverbs 3:7–8   The believer must _____ God always.

3.   How can a person discover God's will? Throughout history, people have employed a variety of methods. How many of these methods have you used to determine God's will for your life (circle the methods you have used)?

The Fleece Method: You make a deal with God by putting out a "fleece," as did Gideon (Judges 6:37–39).

The Fasting Method: You give up food for God. If your motivation is God's will, fasting with prayer works (1 Corinthians 7:5).

The "Flipping Coins" Method: You flip a coin to determine your decision (Proverbs 16:33).

The Feelings Method: Your determine your decision based on emotions (Psalm 27:14).

The "Fishing for Answers" Method: Some believers open their Bible, stick their finger in, and regardless of the context, determine God's will by random readings or by whatever verse their finger lands on (Matthew 27:5; Luke 10:37; John 13:27).

The Default Method: Some believers allow nature to take its course and allow circumstances to determine the outcome (Ephesians 4:14).

The Dreaming Method: Believers ask for a vision (Hebrews 1:1–2).

The Drawing Straws Method: The decision is left to chance (Proverbs 3:5–6).

The Doing Nothing Method: The decision is left to whatever happens (Psalm 37:23; 119:105).

4.   How should a believer determine God's direction and will for his life? Look up each passage of scripture, and determine the method recommended by God.

James 1:5   _____ about it.

Psalm 37:4Be   _____in what interests God.

Proverbs 13:10   _____ to godly people.

Psalm 119:105   Be _____ by God's Word.

Philippians 4:6–7   Make _____ decisions.

5.   Select a decision you must make in your life. Of this decision, ask the following questions:

Will it glorify God?

_____ Yes_____ No_____ Not Sure

Is it consistent with God's Word?

_____ Yes_____ No_____ Not Sure

Will this decision have a positive impact on myself and others?

_____ Yes_____ No_____ Not Sure

Are you positive about the decision? (Do you have God's peace?)

_____ Yes_____ No_____ Not Sure

Will the decision further the cause of Christ?

_____ Yes_____ No_____ Not Sure

Do people I respect agree with my decision?

_____ Yes_____ No_____ Not Sure

Have I prayed about this decision?

_____ Yes_____ No_____ Not Sure

Do I want to reap the fruit of this decision in my future life, in the lives of others, or when Jesus comes again?

_____ Yes_____ No_____ Not Sure

Am I willing to face the results of this decision in the judgment?

_____ Yes_____ No_____ Not Sure

Is this decision God's will for my life?

_____ Yes_____ No_____ Not Sure

6.   Make the following commitments:

Commitment:
From this moment on, I yield myself completely to Jesus Christ.
Signed: _____

From this moment on, I yield my will to the Savior's will.
Signed: _____

From this moment on, I yield my thoughts, words, attitudes, and behaviors to Jesus Christ. (I give Jesus Christ my life.)
Signed: _____

Commitment:
From this moment, I will trust my life to God's sovereign control.
Signed: _____

Commitment:
From this moment on, I will not quench or grieve God's Holy Spirit.
Signed: _____

7.   Describe the level of your commitment to Jesus Christ. (Are you fully yielded to Him?)

8.   "Quench" is an action word. It speaks of putting out a fire. "Grieve" is a love word. (God has emotions. He hurts when believers refuse to do His will.) From the following list, in what ways can believers quench and grieve God's Spirit? ("Quenching" God's Spirit is not doing what God wants you to do. "Grieving" God's Spirit is doing something that God does not want you to do. "Quenching" involves a refusal to do God's will. "Grieving" involves doing something contrary to God's will.) From Old Testament scripture's classic chapter on the history of Israel (Psalm 78), identify ways people can quench or grieve God's Spirit.

Text	Reason God's Spirit Is Quenched/Grieved
Psalm 78:11	When God's people _____ they have a God.
Psalm 78:17	When God's people _____ God to anger.

Psalm 78:18   When God's people _____ (test) God.

Psalm 78:19   When God's people _____ grumble and
                           complain).

Psalm 78: 41   When God's people _____ God.

Psalm 78:56   When God's people do not keep God's commands
                           (disobedience).

9.   Investigate the lives of great Christians. Read their biographies or autobiographies.
      One fascinating study is the life of George Mueller, who ran an orphanage, by faith, in
      Bristol, England. Compare your situation to the lives of the Christians you study. Be
      encouraged by their stories. Apply God's Word to your life.

Z: ZEAL

Jesus Christ had just finished cleansing the temple. Amazed, His disciples remembered that it was written, "The zeal of thine house hath eaten me up" (John 2:17; Psalm 69:9). The purpose of this study is to reexamine the commitments of believers to Jesus Christ. The privilege of every believer is to keep his spiritual commitments current.

1.   The individual Caleb had a zeal for the Lord. From Joshua 14:7–15, examine Caleb's zeal.

2.   The nations Israel and Judah had a zeal for the Lord. From Habakkuk 3:2, comment on their zeal.

3.   How does revival take place? There are ten Old Testament revivals that restored God's zeal to the people of the Lord. Each of those ten Old Testament revivals reveals a condition that must be present for revival to take hold of the hearts of genuine believers and impact society for Jesus Christ. From the following passages of scripture, describe the Old Testament revivals. Determine the key "ingredient" in each revival.

Text	Person(s) under Whom the Revival Took Place	The Revival's Key Ingredient(s)
Genesis 35:2		
Exodus 32:32		
1 Samuel 7:1–13		
1 Kings 18:36–39		
2 Chronicles 7:14		
2 Chronicles 20		
2 Chronicles 30		
2 Chronicles 34–35		
Haggai 1		
Nehemiah 8		

4.　　　Answer the following questions. (Place an X on the appropriate lines.)

Like Caleb, are you wholehearted for the Lord (Joshua 14)?

_____ Yes _____ No _____ My zeal needs improvement

Like Jacob, have you put away (replaced) substitutes for God with the worship of the One True God (Genesis 35:2)?

_____ Yes _____ No _____ My zeal needs improvement

Like Moses, have you confessed your sin (Exodus 32:32)?

_____ Yes _____ No _____ My zeal needs improvement

Like Samuel, do you serve God only (1 Samuel 7:1–13)?

_____ Yes _____ No _____ My zeal needs improvement

Like Elijah, do you let God be God (1 Kings 18:36–39)?

_____ Yes _____ No _____ My zeal needs improvement

Like Asa, do you pray for revival (2 Chronicles 7:14)?

_____ Yes _____ No _____ My zeal needs improvement

Like Jehoshaphat, have you fixed your gaze on God and focused on Him (2 Chronicles 20)?

_____ Yes _____ No _____ My zeal needs improvement

Like Hezekiah, have you repented of known sin (2 Chronicles 30)?

_____ Yes _____ No _____ My zeal needs improvement

Like Josiah, have you rediscovered God's Word? Are you a Word-centered believer (2 Chronicles 34–35)?

_____ Yes _____ No _____ My zeal needs improvement

Like Zerubbabel, have you renewed your interest in God (Haggai 1)?

_____ Yes _____ No _____ My zeal needs improvement

Like Nehemiah, do you rejoice in the Lord (Nehemiah 8:8–10)?

_____ Yes _____ No _____ My zeal needs improvement

Christ came to heal the sick, not the healthy. God can restore your zeal, if you give yourself to Him.

5.   Respond to the following story:

Soren Kierkegaard was a Danish theologian and philosopher. He told this parable:

A wild duck was flying northward with his mate across Europe during springtime. En route, he happened to land in a barnyard in Denmark, where he quickly made friends with the tame ducks that lived there. The wild duck enjoyed the corn and fresh water. He decided to stay for an hour, then for a day, then for a week, and finally, for a month. At the end of that time, he considered flying to join his friends in the vast Northland, but he had begun to enjoy the safety of the barnyard, and the tame ducks had made him feel welcome. So he stayed on for the summer.

One autumn day, when his wild mates were flying toward the south, he heard their quacking. It stirred him with delight, and he enthusiastically flapped his wings and rose into the air to join them. Much to his dismay, he found that he could rise no higher than the eaves of the barn. As he waddled back to the safety of the barnyard, he muttered to himself, "I am satisfied here. I have plenty of food, and the fare is good. Why should I leave?" So he spent the winter on the farm.

In the spring, when the wild ducks flew overhead again, he felt a strange stirring in his heart, but he did not even try to fly up to meet them. When they returned in the fall, they again invited him to rejoin them, but this time the duck did not even notice them. There was stirring in his heart. He simply kept on eating the corn that had made him fat.[20]

Response:

---

[20] A Soren Kierkegaard story referenced by Erwin W. Lutzer, *How in This World Can I Be Holy?* (Chicago, IL: Moody Press, 1974), 7–8.

SPIRITUAL LESSONS FOR GROWING BELIEVERS (DISCIPLESHIP TRAINING)

Perspectives on Discipleship

The Practice of Discipleship

Keith D. Pisani

DISCIPLESHIP TRAINING (SESSION 1)
Perspectives on Discipleship (Study Guide)
As iron sharpens iron, so one man sharpens another.
—Proverbs 27:17

Spiritual growth results when believers disciple other believers. The Bible describes three methods of discipleship. They are the three-legged stool of M_____, the spiritual life (1 Timothy 4:12), M_____ individual believers (Proverbs 27:17), and a formal M of teaching God's Word to others one-on-one, "alongside of," or in group settings.

Churches flourish their people for God.

A disciple is a _____, an _____, and the disciple is an _____ to Jesus Christ.

There is a precedent for discipleship (Matthew 28:18–20).

Since Jesus Christ said "make disciples" (Matthew 28:18–20), what is commanded by Christ must be carried out by Christians. From the following passages, list some examples of people who discipled others:

_____ was evangelized (Acts 9:3–6).
_____ discipled him (Acts 9:10–19).
_____ discipled others (Acts 14:21–23.

_____ was evangelized (Acts 14:19–23).
_____ discipled him (Acts 16:1–5).
_____ discipled others (2 Timothy 2:1, 2).

_____ were evangelized (Acts 18:1, 2).
_____ discipled them (Acts 18:3).
_____ discipled others (Acts 18:24–28).

True discipleship is reproducing the character qualities of Jesus Christ into the lives of others.

Fill in the blanks:

And the things which (your name) _____ has heard from (the name of the person who discipled you) _____, these entrust to (the name of a person you have, are, or will disciple) _____who will teach (the name of a person your disciple will disciple) ____ also. (2 Timothy 2:1, 2)

There are priorities in discipleship (Mark 3:14–15).

Jesus Christ never asks believers to do something that He Himself has not already done. Jesus Christ modeled four priorities in making disciples.

1.   The priority of _____(Matthew 10:2–4; Mark 3:16–19; Luke 6:14–16; Acts 1:13–16)

Jesus Christ took a different approach in the training of His individual disciples. The method Jesus Christ used to disciple the twelve is as follows (from John C. Maxwell's *Developing the Leaders around You*):

Nurtured: Peter, Andrew, James, John, Philip, Nathaniel, Thomas, Matthew, James of Alphaeus, Thaddaeus, Simon the Zealot, Judas Iscariot

Equipped: Peter, Andrew, James, John, Philip, Nathaniel, Thomas, Matthew

Developed: Peter, Andrew, James, John

Nurtured	**Equipped**	**Developed**
All	Some	A few
Focused on needs	Focused on tasks	Focused on the person
Prepared for service	Prepared for management	Prepared to lead
Maintain their ministries	Add to their ministries	Multiply their ministries
Jesus Christ helped them	Jesus Christ taught them	Jesus Christ mentored them
Jesus Christ established them	Jesus Christ released them	Jesus Christ empowered them
Jesus Christ gave them what they wanted	Jesus Christ gave them what the ministry needed	Jesus Christ gave them what they needed
Need-oriented	Task-oriented	Character oriented

Little growth in ministries	Short-term growth in ministries	Long-term growth in ministries
Bore some fruit	Bore more fruit	Bore much fruit

How were the disciples of Jesus Christ prepared to follow Him?

2.   The priority of _____ (John 1:6–8; Mark 1:16–20; Matthew 10:1–7)

         Prepared by _____ (Matthew 4:18–19; John 1:6–8)

         Prepared by _____ (Mark 1:16–20)

         Prepared by _____ (Matthew 10:1–7)

3.   The priority of (Mark 3:14, 15)

         The disciple's greatest priority is s_____ t_____with Jesus.

4.   The priority of _____.(John 15:8)

         Every disciple should _____.(John 15:8)

         Every disciple should _____.(John 13:35)

         Every disciple should _____.(John 8:31, 32)

         Every disciple should _____.(Luke 14:33)

         Every disciple should _____.(Luke 14:26)

         Every disciple should _____.(Matthew 16:24)

Notes

THE PRACTICE OF DISCIPLESHIP (STUDY GUIDE)

You therefore, my son, be strong in the grace that is in Christ Jesus. And
the things that you have heard from me among many witnesses, commit
these to faithful men who will be able to teach others also.
—2 Timothy 2:1–2

Since Paul wrote that what believers are taught should be taught to others (2 Timothy 2:1–2),
how should believers disciple other believers? Scripture reveals three methods of discipleship.

Modeling the Spiritual Life (1 Timothy 4:12)

The "as He" passages in 1 John reveal seven examples of how disciplers should model
the life and teachings of Jesus Christ.

1 John 1:7   Develop biblical. _____

1 John 2:6   Make your relationship with Jesus Christ a daily _____

1 John 3:2   _____ as if Jesus could come today.

1 John 3:3   Submit to God's _____ fire and _____ pure.

1 John 3:7   Live _____by living the Christ life before others.

1 John 3:23   _____ like Jesus loves.

1 John 4:17   Seek eternal _____ to present to Jesus in the day of
judgment.

People do what people see. More is caught than taught. When believers model the character
qualities of Christ before others, believers influence others to grow.

2.   Currently, what principles of modeling Jesus Christ do you practice?

3.   In order to be a Christlike model, which of the principles do you need to further
develop in your life?

Mentoring Individual Believers (Proverbs 27:17)

1.   Since mentors are relational, what work do mentors perform in the lives of others?

      Mentors _____

2.   By what character traits should mentors by known?

3.   Where can believers mentor other believers?

      A_____ and at A_____

4.   What mentoring relationships are found in scripture?

Passage	Mentor(s)	Mentoring Focus
Exodus 18		
Deuteronomy 31:1–8; 34:9		
Numbers 13; 14:6–9; 34:16–19; Joshua 14:6–15		
1 Samuel 9–15		
1 Samuel 16; 19:18–24		
1 Samuel 18:1–4; 19:1–7; 20:1–42		
1 Kings 19:16–21; 2 Kings 2:1–16; 3:11		
2 Chronicles 24:1–25		
Acts 4:36–37; 9:26–30; 11:22–30		
Acts 15:36–39; 2 Timothy 4:11		
Acts 18:1–3, 24–28		
Acts 16:1–3; Philippians 2:19–23; 1 and 2 Timothy		

2 Corinthians 7:6, 13–15;
8:17; Titus

Galatians 3:24–25

5.   Make a list of people you can mentor.

_____ _____ _____

Ministering Discipleship to Others (1 Timothy 2:1–7; Acts 14:21–23)

In order to disciple, a believer must know what he should be, and he should know what he should do. Two passages provide assistance in establishing what disciplers should be and what disciplers should do.

1. The discipler should be faithful to the _____ entrusted to him (2 Timothy 2:1–7).

Discipleship is a process of r____ that leads to
g____ and spiritual m_____.

Believers should disciple like a master _____ (2 Timothy 2:15).

Disciplers should be_____ like a _____ (2 Timothy 2:3–4).

Disciplers should be _____ like an _____ (2 Timothy 2:5).

Disciplers should be_____ like a _____ (2 Timothy 2:6).

2. The discipler follows a _____ of action (Acts 14:21–23).

There are six steps on the stairway to discipleship. Once these six steps are accomplished, the person discipled can start with step 1, repeat the steps, and disciple someone himself.

Acts 14:21   E_____ (Getting Up)

Acts 14:21   E_____(Following Up)

Acts 14:22   E_____(Shoring Up)

Acts 14:22   E_____(Looking Up)

Acts 14:23   E_____(Signing Up)

Acts 14:23   E_____(Growing Up

To discover how the early church grew, see Acts 2:41; 2:42; 2:47; 4:4; 5:14; 6:1; 12:24; 16:5.

CERTIFICATE OF COMPLETION

Spiritual Lessons for Growing Believers
A to Z Studies (26 Sessions)
Dr. Keith D. Pisani (Author)

This is to certify that

_____

(Name of Participant)

has completed *The Spiritual Lessons for Growing Believers 26-Session "A to Z" Studies.*

Date: _____

Official Signature of Discipler

_____

But grow in grace, and in the knowledge of our Lord and Savior Jesus
Christ. To Him be glory both now and forever. Amen.
—2 Peter 3:18

SELECTED BIBLIOGRAPHY

(As Listed in the Companion Book
Spiritual Lessons for Growing Believers)

Abbott, Carl. *Disciples in Deed.* Cleveland, OH: Baptist Mid-Missions, 1993.

Adams, Jay E. *Prayers for Troubled Times.* Grand Rapids: Baker, 1979.

Adsit, Christopher B. *Personal Disciple-Making.* Nashville, TN: Thomas Nelson Publishers, 1993.

Aldrich, Joseph E. *Life-Style Evangelism.* Portland: Multnomah Press, 1981.

Allen, Ronald B., and Gordon Borror. *Worship: Rediscovering the Missing Jewel.* Portland: Multnomah Press, 1982.

Bailey, Robert W. *New Ways in Christian Worship.* Nashville: Broadman, 1981.

Barber, Cyril J., and Gary H. Strauss. *Leadership.* Nashville: Broadman, 1968.

Barry, James C., and Gulledge. *Ideas for Effective Worship Services.* Nashville: Broadman Press, n.d.

Beabout, Florence M. *New Life for Boys and Girls.* Denver: Accent Publications, 1976.

Belt, Maynard. *Discipleship.* Elyria, OH: Baptist Mission of North America, 1987.

Bisagno, John R. *How to Build an Evangelistic Church.* Nashville: Broadman.

Blanchard, Charles A. *Getting Things from God.* Wheaton, IL: Victor Books, 1989.

Bounds, E. M. *Power through Prayer.* Grand Rapids: Zondervan, 1965.

_____. *Prayer and Praying Men.* Grand Rapids: Baker, 1921.

_____. *Purpose in Prayer.* Grand Rapids: Baker, 1920.

_____. *The Best of E. M. Bounds.* Grand Rapids: Baker, 1981.

_____. *The Essentials of Prayer.* Grand Rapids: Baker, 1925.

_____. *The Necessity of Prayer.* Grand Rapids: Baker, n.d.

_____. *The Possibilities of Prayer.* Grand Rapids: Baker, 1923.

_____. *The Reality of Prayer.* Grand Rapids: Baker, 1924.

_____. *The Weapon of Prayer.* Grand Rapids: Baker, 1931.

Bridges, Jerry. *The Pursuit of Holiness.* Colorado Springs, CO: NavPress, 1978.

Brock, Fred R. *The Power of Prayer.* Schaumburg, IL: Regular Baptist Press, 1985.

Bubna, Donald, and Sarah Rickets. *Building People through a Caring Sharing Fellowship.* Wheaton: Tyndale, 1978.

Burch, Charles H. *A Personal Follow-Up for New Converts.* Clarks Summit, PA: Baptist Bible College of Pennsylvania, 1989.

Burns, Ralph O. *Basic Bible Truths for New Christians.* Schaumburg, IL: Regular Baptist Press, 1971.

"Centurio Sempronis." Wikipedia: The Free Encyclopedia. Wikimedia Foundation, Inc., November 23, 2015. Web. January 2, 2016. <http://en.wikipedia.org/wiki/Centurio Sempronis>.

Chambers, J. Oswald. *My Utmost for His Highest.* New York: Dodd, Mead, and Company, 1935.

Coleman, Robert E. *The Master Plan of Evangelism.* Old Tappan, NJ: Fleming H. Revell, 1964.

Cook, Robert A. *Now That I Believe.* Chicago: Moody, 1977.

Dean, Jerry, and Hanrick, Frank. *Milk, Meat, Bread, and Fish.* Rocky Mount, NC: Positive Action for Christ, 1972.

Drummond, Lewis. *Leading Your Church in Evangelism.* Nashville: Broadman, n.d.

Eims, LeRoy. *Be the Leader You Were Meant to Be.* Wheaton, IL: Scripture Press, 1975.

_____. *The Lost Art of Disciple Making.* Grand Rapids, MI: Zondervan, 1978.

Feather, R. Ethel. *Outreach Evangelism in the Sunday School.* Nashville: Convention, n.d.

Fortune, Don and Katie. *Discover Your God Given Gifts.* Grand Rapids, MI: Chosen Books, 1987.

_____. *Discover Your Motivational Gift.* Kingston, WA: Don and Katie Fortune, 1978.

_____. *Discover Your Motivational Gift Adult Testing Sheets*. Kingston, WA: Don and Katie Fortune, 1978.

Fryling, Alice. *Disciplemakers Handbook*. Downers Grove, IL: InterVarsity Press, 1989.

Gangel, Kenneth O. *Building Leaders for Church Education*. Chicago: Moody, 1981.

Getz, Gene. *Building Up One Another*. Wheaton, IL: Victor Books, 1973.

Godfrey, George. *How to Win Souls and Influence People for Heaven*. Kearney, NE: Morris Publishing, 1973.

Goetz, David L., ed. *Building Church Leaders*. Chicago, IL: Christianity Today, 1998.

Green, Larry D. "The Indispensable Skills of Effective Leadership." *The Church Planter*. (1999): 18.7.

Gromacki, Robert. *Salvation Is Forever*. Chicago: Moody Press, 1973.

Haldidian, Allen. *Discipleship: Helping Other Christians Grow*. Chicago: Moody, 1987.

Hamrick, Frank and Jerry Dean. *Milk, Meat, Bread, and Fish*. Rocky Mount, NC: Positive Action for Christ, 1973.

Hanks Jr., Billie. *Everyday Evangelism: How to Do It and How to Teach It*. Grand Rapids: Zondervan, 1982.

Hart, Archibald. "Am I an Ethical Leader?" *Building Church Leaders*. (1998): 2.4.

Hiebert, D. Edmond. "An Expository Study of Matthew 28:16–20." *Bibliotheca Sacra*. 149 (1992): 338–354.

Henrichsen, Walter A. *Disciples Are Made Not Born*. Wheaton, IL: Victor Books, 1988.

Hendricks, Howard and William. *As Iron Sharpens Iron*. Chicago: Moody Press, 1995.

_____. *Say It with Love*. Wheaton, IL: Victor, 1979.

Hocking, David. *1 John*. La Mirada, CA: Biola University, 1990.

_____. *Perspectives on Prayer*. Orange, CA: Promise Publishing Company, 1989.

_____. *Spiritual Gifts*. Orange, CA: Promise Publishing Company, 1989.

The Holy Bible. The King James Version.

_____. The New International Version.

Homer. *The Odyssey*. Translated by Samuel Butler. New York: Barnes and Noble, 1993.

Hughes, R. Kent. *Disciplines of a Godly Man*. Wheaton, IL: Crossway Books, 1991.

Hull, Bill. *Jesus Christ Disciple Maker*. Grand Rapids, MI: Fleming H. Revell, 1978.

_____. *The Disciple Making Church*. Grand Rapids, MI: Fleming H. Revell, 1984.

_____. *The Disciple Making Pastor*. Grand Rapids, MI: Fleming H. Revell, 1984.

Hybles, Bill, and Mark Mittleberg. *Becoming a Contagious Christian*. Grand Rapids, MI: Zondervan, 1994.

Jackson, Mark. *Ready, Set, Grow!* Schaumburg, IL: Regular Baptist Press, 1989.

_____. *The Doctrine and Administration of the Local Church*. Schaumburg, IL: Regular Baptist Press, 1980.

Johnson, Carl. "Whom Are You Doubting?" *Encyclopedia of 7700 Illustrations*. (1979): 1190–1191.

Johnson, Irvin. *TELL: Training Evangelistic Lay Leaders*. North Tonawanda, NY: First Baptist Church.

Keller, W. Phillip. *A Layman Looks at the Lord's Prayer*. Chicago: Moody, 1976.

Kennedy, James. *Evangelism Explosion*. Wheaton: Tyndale, 1996.

Kittel, Gerhard, ed. *Theological Dictionary of the New Testament*. Grand Rapids, MI: William B. Eerdmans Publishing Company, 1967. S.v. "enkratees," by Walter Grundmann. 2:339.

_____. *Theological Dictionary of the New Testament*. Grand Rapids, MI: William B. Eerdmans Publishing Company, 1967. S.v. "manthano," by K. H. Rengstorf. 4:390.

_____. *Theological Dictionary of the New Testament*. Grand Rapids, MI: William B. Eerdmans Publishing Company, 1967. S.v. "poimaino," by Joachim Jeremias. 6:485.

_____. *Theological Dictionary of the New Testament*. Grand Rapids, MI: William B. Eerdmans Publishing Company, 1967. S.v. "steerizo," by Gunther Harder. 7:653.

_____. *Theological Dictionary of the New Testament*. Grand Rapids, MI: William B. Eerdmans Publishing Company, 1967. S.v. "tupos," by Leonard Goppelt. 8:246.

Kroll, J. Woodrow. *10 First Steps for the New Christian*. Lincoln, NE: Back through the Bible, 1992.

Kuhne, Gary W. *The Dynamics of Discipleship Training*. Grand Rapids, MI: Zondervan, 1978.

_____. *The Dynamics of Personal Follow-Up*. Grand Rapids, MI: Zondervan, 1976.

Lacock, Melvin. *Won by One*. Des Moines, IO: Bible Press, 1978.

Lau-Lavie, Naphtali. *Moshe Dayan*. Hartford, CN: Hartmore House, 1968.

Lee Tan, Paul. *Encyclopedia of 7700 Illustrations*. Rockville, MD: Assurance Publishers, 1979.

Lewis, C. S. *Mere Christianity*. New York: Macmillan, 1970.

Lewis, Larry. *Organize to Evangelize*. Nashville: Broadman.

Little, Paul E. *How to Give Away Your Faith*. Downers Grove, IL: InterVarsity Press, 1966.

_____. *Know What You Believe*. Wheaton, IL: Victor Books, 1987.

_____. *Know Why You Believe*. Wheaton, IL: Victor Books, 1980.

Lockyer, Herbert. *All the Prayers of the Bible*. Grand Rapids: Zondervan, 1966.

Luter, A. Boyd. "Discipleship and the Church." *Bibliotheca Sacra*. 137 (1980): 267–273.

Lutzer, Erwin W. *How in This World Can I Be Holy?* Chicago: Moody Press, 1974.

MacArthur, John. *The Master's Plan for the Church*. Chicago: Moody, 1981.

MacArthur Jr., John. *The Ultimate Priority*. Chicago: Moody, 1983.

Macauley, J. C., and Robert H. Belton. *Personal Evangelism*. Chicago: Moody, 1956.

Marsh, F. E. *The Discipler's Manual*. Grand Rapids, MI: Kregel Publications, 1991.

Maxwell, John C. *Developing the Leader within You*. Wheaton, IL: Victor Books, 1980.

_____. *Developing the Leaders around You*. Nashville: Nelson, 1993.

_____. *The 21 Irrefutable Laws of Leadership*. Nashville, TN: Thomas Nelson, 1998.

McPhee, Arthur G. *Friendship Evangelism*. Grand Rapids: Zondervan, 1978.

Miller, Joseph. *Discovering Life in the Church.* Schaumburg, IL: Regular Baptist Press, n.d.

_____. *The Church Planter.* Palm Beach Gardens, FL: Discovering Life Ministries, 1992.

Miller, Vernon, ed. *Basic Training.* Schaumburg, IL: Regular Baptist Press, 1993.

Moody, D. L. *Prevailing Prayer.* Chicago: Moody, n.d.

Morgan, G. Campbell. *Discipleship.* Grand Rapids, MI: Baker, 1973.

_____. *Evangelism.* Grand Rapids, MI: Baker, 1976.

Morrissey, Kirkie. *On Holy Ground.* Colorado Springs, CO: NavPress, 1983.

Murray, Andrew. *The Ministry of Intercessory Prayer.* Minneapolis, MN: Bethany House, 1981.

_____. *The Prayer Life.* Chicago: Moody, n.d.

Olford, Stephen F. "The Essentials of Biblical Leadership." *Luther Rice Lecture Series.* January (1999): 1–2.

Ortlund, Anne. *Up with Worship.* Glendale, CA: Regal Publications, 1975.

Pentecost, J. Dwight. *Design for Discipleship.* Grand Rapids, MI: Kregel Publications, 1996.

Peterson, Jim. *Evangelism as a Lifestyle.* Colorado Springs: NavPress, 1980.

_____. *Lifestyle Discipleship.* Colorado Springs, CO: NavPress, 1993.

Phillips, John. *Exploring Romans.* Neptune, NJ: Loizeaux Brothers, 1991.

Pickering, Ernest. *The Theology of Evangelism.* Clarks Summit, PA: Baptist Bible College Press, 1974.

Pisani, Keith D. Sermons preached.

Richards, Larry. *Born to Grow.* Wheaton, IL: Victor Books, 1977.

Riggs, Charlie. *Learning to Walk with God.* Minneapolis, MN: World Wide Publications, 1986.

Sanders, J. Oswald. *Shoe Leather Commitment.* Chicago, IL: Moody, 1990.

_____. *Spiritual Discipleship.* Chicago: Moody, 1994.

_____. *Spiritual Leadership.* Chicago: Moody, 1967.

Santhouse, Paul, ed. *Design for Discipleship*. Colorado Springs, CO: NavPress, 1980.

_____. *Discipleship Journal*. Colorado Springs, CO: NavPress.

_____. *Growing as a Christian*. Colorado Springs, CO: NavPress, 1964.

_____. *Growing in Christ*. Colorado Springs, CO: NavPress, 1992.

Scroggie, W. Graham. *How to Pray*. Grand Rapids: Kregel, 1981.

Shedd, Charlie. *How to Develop a Praying Church*. Nashville: Abingdon Press, 1964.

Sisson, Richard. *Training for Evangelism*. Chicago: Moody, 1979.

Smith, Alfred B., ed. *Living Hymns*. Montrose, PA: Encore Publications, 1979.

Smith, Fred. "Conducting a Spiritual Audit." *Building Church Leaders* (1998): 2.5.

_____. "How to Find a Mentor." *Leadership*. Winter (1999): 57–58.

_____. "Mentoring That Matters." *Leadership*. Winter (1999): 94–98.

Spurgeon, Charles Haddon. *The Soul Winner*. Grand Rapids, MI: Wm. B. Eerdmans Publishing Company, 1963.

Stanford, Miles J. *Principles of Spiritual Growth*. Lincoln, NE: Back to the Bible, 1972.

Stanley, Charles. *The Glorious Journey*. Nashville, TN: Thomas Nelson Publishers, 1996.

Steadman, Ray C. *Body Life*. Glendale, CA: Regal Publications, 1972.

Stoutenburg, Dennis C. "Out of My Sight!" "Get Thee behind Me!" or "Follow after Me!": There Is No Choice in God's Kingdom." *The Journal of Evangelical Theology*. 36:2 (1993): 173–178.

Swindoll, Charles. "What I Want to Be When I Grow Up." *Leadership*. Summer (1999): 59.

Torrey, R. A., *How to Pray*. Chicago: Moody, n.d.

Tozer, A. W. *Keys to the Deeper Life*. Grand Rapids, MI: Zondervan, 1957.

Turabian, Kate L. *A Manual for Writers*, 6th ed. Chicago: University of Chicago Press, 1993.

Van Zuylen, Dirk C. "Discipling Like Jesus." In *Discipleship Journal*. 110 (1999): 76–80.

Vines, Jerry. Wanted: *Soul Winners*. Nashville, Broadman.

Ware, Gene. *You Can Make Disciples*. Waco, TX: Word Books,1978.

Warren, Rick. *The Purpose Driven Church*. Grand Rapids, MI: Zondervan, 1995.

Watters, Philip. *The Prayers of the Bible*. Grand Rapids: Baker, 1959.

Wiersbe, Warren. *Classic Sermons on Prayer*. Grand Rapids: Kregel, 1987.

_____. "When No One Is Looking." *Building Church Leaders* (1998): 2.11.

_____. *Real Worship*. Nashville: Oliver Nelson, 1986.